NETWORKING FOR HEALERS

CURATING THE CONVERSATIONS, CONNECTIONS, AND COMMUNITY THAT MANIFEST YOUR DREAM BUSINESS

LAURA DI FRANCO

NETWORKING FOR HEALERS

CURATING THE CONVERSATIONS, CONNECTIONS,
AND COMMUNITY THAT MANIFEST
YOUR DREAM BUSINESS

LAURA DI FRANCO

Dedication

To all the healers who hate networking:
What else is possible?

Want to network with a community of badass healers who will help you grow your business?

Join us in Brave Badass Healers,
a Community for World-Changers on Facebook,
and watch the transformation begin.
Enjoy two free events a month:
https://www.Facebook.com/YourHighVibeBusiness/

Table of Contents

Part 2

The Art of Juicy Conversations

Part 3

Making Connections that Grow Your Business

Part 4

How to Share Your Business and Offerings Like a Badass

Chapter 16 | 80

When is it a Sales Conversation?

Chapter 17 | 85

How to Curate High-Vibe Sales Conversation Energy

Chapter 18 | 88

How to Know When to Cut it Short and Move On (Objections)

Chapter 19 | 92

How to Close a Sales Conversation with Ease and Grace

Chapter 20 | 99

The Important Difference Between Introductions and Referrals

Part 5

Now What?

Introduction

I'm going to start this party by sharing a story about the day I signed up for an in-person networking event and left vowing never to network again.

It was a local luncheon networking event with a price tag, and I was ready to pay to play for a new experience. The lunch was okay, but because I was nervous about meeting a bunch of people I didn't know, I barely ate, especially the salad, because when those leafy greens get stuck in your teeth, and you don't have your BFF with you to say, "Hey girl, you got something in your teeth," well, I would rather be hungry.

The luncheon showcased a keynote speaker and a few other member speakers and then roundtable networking. I had my business cards ready.

I entered and perused the room, talked to a couple of people who were manning their sponsor tables, and ran into a couple of people I knew from another network. The two people I knew graced me with a version of "Hey Laura, nice to see you here," but quickly ran off to other tables.

Why aren't they wanting to sit with me?

I sat at a table with people I didn't know for the main event. I wished so badly one of those ladies would've invited me to their table. The self-sabotage set in and was relentless throughout the event.

NOTE: If you see a newbie arrive at an event you're a regular at, make it a point to greet them and ask them to sit with you. Or introduce them to a friend or other newbie and help them connect.

I began listening to the speaker and was focused on her until people at my table started whisper-talking to each other, making it impossible to hear. I wasn't brave enough to "shush" people I didn't know, so I sat there, getting more frustrated as time went on. I heard one of the regulars finally butt in with a "Shush!"

Thank goodness!

When it came time to do our roundtable intros, I remember my heart beating out of my chest so hard the entire time others were doing their intros that I barely listened to them. And because several people at the table did not respect the 60-second rule we were given, the couple of us that went last didn't have enough time, and we were interrupted by the host, "Okay ladies, wrap it up!"

Fuck. Really?

I'm going to make a longer sob story shorter for you now.

That day was my proof that networking sucked and that I wasn't cut out for it. I never went back to that meeting and didn't do any formal networking for many years afterward.

Enter Donnie Boivin and his one-liner that began reshaping the way I thought about networking: "This isn't about selling your shit. It's about helping other people build their businesses."

The idea changed everything for me, and I dove head first into learning more and eventually wanted to teach these better networking principles to my healer audience.

That one idea changed my thoughts, energy, intentions, conversations, and behaviors. It started to help me grow my business into an empire. And here we are now. Welcome to *Networking for Healers*!

Becoming a connector and badass networker is the fast track to growing your business, but you're thinking: *Can I do that? I hate networking. Don't make me, I'm an introvert!*

I'm so excited to share this book with you. I want you to love networking like I do.

You'll have to unlearn a thing or two, though. Because what you've been taught about networking is all wrong. Or at least, if you've tried all the things and still hate it, there's a reason, and there's a better way.

Get ready to have your mind blown about what's possible when you create genuine, powerful relationships with people who want to help you build your business and for whom you want to do the same thing.

It's not about you, actually. It's about what you can do for them. And when you realize the "secrets" to this, everything will fall into place, and you'll be so excited to expand your network! I was so excited I decided to write this book about it!

Even if peopling makes your head spin and that heavy pit of dread hangs in your gut, I promise there's a huge transformation in store if you're willing to open your mind and heart to getting to know people.

This book is for you if you're a holistic healer, health and wellness practitioner, author, or entrepreneur who wants to:

1. Come out of your shell, feel more confident, and learn how to share yourself and what you do with others in an authentic way that leaves you feeling great.

2. Learn the art and soul of connecting and building long-lasting relationships and partnerships that grow your business.

3. Learn how to create a networking conversation that lights you (and them) up.

4. Go from being a connector to a super-connector.

5. Grow your business faster.

6. Build a business-building community that helps everyone thrive.

7. Sell more of your services or offerings and increase your income.

8. Expand your community and business and create powerful collaborations and joint venture partnerships.

9. Leave your legacy in a more impactful way.

10. Love networking! And who doesn't want more love in their life?

Let's do this!

PS. Throughout the book, you'll see two symbols.

 The pot of gold is where I'm dropping one of the golden nuggets I want you to remember.

 And the megaphone is where I'm giving you a script you can practice with your networking partners. Enjoy!

Part 1

The Secrets and Superpowers of Connecting

You must get your energy, intention, and mindset right before you dive in. The secrets of networking are no different than in healing. It's about awareness. Use what you already know, and let me help you apply it to building relationships that build your business

Let's get to it!

Chapter 1

Your Mindset, Energy, and Intention

Oh my goodness—brave business networking! I'm really excited to be here with all of you, sharing the secrets of networking. Thank you for reading and for being interested in something that'll completely change your life and business. That's what it's done for me.

These first few chapters are some foundational steps you need to make everything shift in your world of networking.

First, imagine this. I'm sitting on my patio in the late summer. It's just starting to feel like a hint of fall in the air. A few leaves are falling, and it's cool enough to sit out there without sweating through my clothes. As I sip my espresso, take deep breaths of gratitude, and watch the shimmery leaves as the sun rises, thoughts of NETWORKING slide in!

It's hard to slow my mind down sometimes, especially when it comes to business, because my business is such a part of my purposeful life that the Universe caught on a while ago and started pushing downloads into my mornings.

If you've never heard the term *download* as it relates to receiving messages from the Universe, then you haven't been hanging with my healer friends enough!

This particular morning, an entire networking course moved through me. I found myself running inside to pop open my laptop and catch the four-session course agenda before it was lost into the ethers.

I created some basic graphics on Canva, wrote up some copy to share with my peeps, and posted it in my Brave Badass Healers, a Community for World-Changers group on Facebook. In about a day, there were 45 people signed up.

Whoa! Okay, Universe, I'm paying attention.

Welcome to this new BETA course—Brave Business Networking—in the book version.

I have a passion for this thing I wanna teach you, and I want to make it completely easy for you to invest in yourself. It's why I decided to write a book after I taught the course.

If some of you remember, I sold this course for the price of a book. That was part of the download. I wanted to sell a few copies of two other books I've written for you: *How to Have Fun with Your Fear* and *The Brave Healer Business Mindset Transformation Journal.*

Honestly, I thought this idea was so brilliant. Because those books are packed with more information that'll change your life and business. And as an author, I'm always going to be wanting to share my books with the world. This was a double whammy awesomeness—the course for a book sale! Win-win!

To those of you who accepted that offer and purchased one of my books: Thank you so much! Thank you to everyone who attended the course and took action! I'm so honored to be on this journey with all of you.

Now, get ready to take what you learn and run with it, y'all. I pay everything forward. I want you to know everything. There are no secrets. There's just what works for you.

The fact that you're here tells me there's something about networking you need and want that you're interested in and that feels good to you. Or maybe it feels a little scary, and you're hoping I'll help with that, which I'm totally going to do.

Like I said before, I hated networking. I didn't like the energy, and I didn't get any business from it.

Well, duh. I was sitting there with that awful energy, right? There are obvious differences between online networking and in-person networking, but there's no difference in how you show up with the energy and intention you want to attract more of. Getting to know people and building relationships is badass.

Your success in business relies upon people. You gotta love them. You gotta want to genuinely get to know them. They're the ones handing you their credit card. People are the reason you're successful or not. So, it behooves everyone to get interested in and good at this. I've been able to build my current business, Brave Healer Productions, by building relationships that mean a lot to me.

Up until now, I'm referring to relationships with clients, but I also love building them with strategic business partners and dreaming up powerful collaborations. That's another level of badassery.

I want you to have an idea of what's possible. I want you to ask yourself that question. Go ahead and ask yourself: "Self, what else is possible here?" And then sit with the question without attaching to getting an immediate answer. You healers understand the power of that tool. Now it's time to practice it for networking.

Curate Your Energy

Deep breath, everyone. Drop down, ground, and center yourself in the energy you want to attract. Do it now as you're reading. You might ask yourself: *What else is possible for my business?* Fill yourself up with gratitude, excitement, and possibility. What other kinds of energy do you or your business need? Call it in right now.

If you hate networking, think about what you're setting yourself up for. Use the strategies you already know about manifestation and healing, and use them for networking!

I prep for networking activities by doing this energy curation first. Y'all have heard me say something similar when it comes to writing: What do you want them to feel? Excited? Well, how do *you* feel today? Tired? Excited isn't happening, then. So, maybe take three deep breaths and get yourself excited. Ask yourself exciting questions. With awareness, we have the choice to create a higher vibe. And we *must* do this for our networking activities!

Work on Your Mindset

I love asking mind-shifting questions. *What else is possible today? What if I meet someone who changes my business or life today? What if I learn something today that I've never learned before that changes everything?* That's exciting! And I can get myself into that excited state with one or two questions and two deep breaths. You don't need 30 minutes. It can be instantaneous!

What energy are you showing up with today? What do you want to attract more of?

PRACTICAL TIP: The other preparation I make doesn't look like much, but it really helps. I have my contact info ready to go to make it super easy for people to connect with me, no matter if I'm in person or online.

Online meetings: When I go to an online networking meeting, I have a document pulled up on my computer with my contact information typed out. All I have to do is copy, paste, enter, and be done! I include the name of my company, what I do, and whom I serve ("Publishing for holistic health and wellness professionals" speaks directly to my ideal client), and then I include my website, making sure to type that (and any) links with the HTTPS://. That way, you can click on that blue line of the link, and it'll come up on your computer. Then, I include any other contact information I want to offer (Email address, cell number, LinkedIn profile link, etc.).

Here's an example of my copy/paste contact info:

Laura Di Franco, CEO of Brave Healer Productions
Publishing for holistic health and wellness professionals
https://lauradifranco.com
Email: support@LauraDiFranco.com
LinkedIn: https://www.linkedin.com/in/laura-di-franco-1b037a5/

When you don't have this already typed somewhere, and you try to type your info in the Zoom chat and hit 'enter' one line at a time, you create multiple messages in the chat instead of one. That's annoying.

I keep a couple of strategic documents up on my computer for every online networking meeting. I review them before the day's or week's meetings because maybe this week we're launching a book, and I want to have the Amazon link ready and clickable. You can change it as you see fit.

PRACTICAL TIP: Create and use a tracking spreadsheet. I'm going to cover this in more detail in Chapter 12. For now, make a basic spreadsheet or make sure to keep track of your conversations in a notebook—whichever is easier.

This is all great so far, and I hope you are starting to get excited about this, but what are we doing here anyhow? What is the goal of all this?

 The goal of networking conversations is to help our friends build their businesses.

If this is the first time you've heard this definition of networking and you're thinking, *wait, Laura, I thought this was about building my business,* then I want you to take a long, deep breath and pause.

Let me explain it this way: You're here to help somebody else build their business. When you become a connector, and you're genuinely building relationships and getting to know other people to the point you can think of someone to introduce them to, the world starts to open up for you. It is because of the high level of energy you're practicing. When you take a genuine interest in those you are connecting with, so much of that beautiful energy will come back to you. And believe me, your business will grow.

I started asking myself:

What can I do for them?

How can I help them get the word out?

How can I be a champion of their legacy?

I'll share a lot more about these connections and how to go about this, but that's the basic goal: helping *them* build their business.

Let's look at this idea another way:

What energy and intention are you showing up with? Is it to sell your shit or help them? Do a gut check on this immediately!

How can you get yourself to that desired state of energy you want to be in today? How can you get yourself excited about this? How can you help your networking partners?

The next thing to work on is how to ask great questions of our partners that will result in a know-love-trust relationship. How are we going to get to know them at the next level? It's never too late to make a best friend or a powerful business partner or collaborator. What if you went into networking with a curiosity about who your next best friend in life might be? Ooh, I love that! Let's get to the badass question asking.

Chapter 2

How to Ask Great Questions

What if you went into networking with a curiosity about who your next best friend in life might be? Yes, I repeated the question because I really want you to understand what networking can do for you.

Before I met Donnie Boivin, the founder of Success Champion Networking, I built a strong community of healers, and we were doing all kinds of events and get-togethers. Donnie found me and invited me on his podcast. The podcast was his first layer of relationship-building and networking at the time. He asked me to be a guest, and the rest is history. He gave before he asked. We got to know each other and immediately hit it off in terms of business collaboration. On that first networking call, he asked me, "What's your story?" He was interested in me. And he listened and asked great questions.

Donnie and I have co-authored two books together, have co-led masterminds and workshops, and I now run a chapter of Success Champion Networking for him here in Bethesda, Maryland, called The Bethesda Badasses. I've also spoken at his business summit.

If I hadn't gone into that first conversation with that 'what's possible' mindset, I may have closed myself off to a crap ton of opportunities. And, most importantly, Donnie's business grew and so did mine!

What if the next powerful business partnership you create with somebody creates a stream of income you weren't even thinking of?

That's fun stuff. That's the kind of stuff I'm talking about. It all starts with understanding how to ask great questions that build a know-love-trust relationship with your networking partner and show them you're genuinely interested in getting to know them and what they do.

After meeting Donnie and getting involved in some of the networking education he was offering, I realized that networking was already about something I loved to do: Help people! I just wasn't thinking about it in that way. I was thinking about networking in terms of how to sell my shit. That was the wrong strategy and horrible energy. Since shifting this, I can honestly say networking has become one of my favorite business and life-building things to do.

Learn to Ask Great Questions

What questions will help you to get to know people at the next level and understand who to introduce them to? Which questions will help you get so clear about what they do, that you say "Oh my gosh, I gotta introduce you to so and so." Also, how can you find the passion inside them? Great questions will uncover their passion and their why.

A strategic move in networking with me is to understand the kinds of goals and passions I have. And I need to figure out what your goals and passions are.

What matters to you right now? That's a great question to ask everybody you meet!

What are you passionate about? It's going to be a good conversation because the energy will be behind it.

Who would you like to be introduced to? Many people forget to ask this most basic question. And, folks, be prepared to answer it, too!

Sometimes, you have to ask clarifying questions if you're confused or unclear so that you can make the best possible introductions. More about this later.

Chapter 3

Clarifying Questions

"Tell me about what you do" is a good way to start off the conversation.

You can add, **"Tell me about your ideal client."** And notice, these aren't questions. They are statements that invite your partner to begin to describe things. They are open-ended on purpose.

Do you even know who your ideal client is? Do you know how to answer that question? It will truly serve you to understand how to answer this question, and it takes some practice.

We all need practice. Make sure to scan the resources later in the book because practice makes perfect, and I'm going to give you a bunch of ideas for safe, amazing networking spaces to go practice in. For now, remember to join Brave Badass Healers, a Community for World-Changers on Facebook—it's where we do our Monday Morning Breakthroughs business development and networking events! Find it at https://www.Facebook.com/YourHighVibeBusiness/

It doesn't matter who you are; we all need to practice talking about ourselves in a way that the other person gets it and gets clear on who we want to be introduced to. It's a two-way street. We need to have the ability to ask super-awesome questions and the ability to talk about ourselves, both in order to generate great intros for each.

Here's an example:

If you were to ask me today what I'm passionate about, I might say: "We're taking a group of authors to New York to retreat for four nights, and then we're going to write two books together. If you know a holistic health and wellness practitioner who wants to become a published author with us and wants to come to the Honor's Haven Retreat Center and play for four days and do some deep healing work and writing together, please send them my way."

Right now, that's an amazing introduction for me. It's pretty specific. You guys know who I'm talking about because it's all of you, right? You might have friends who aren't published yet who keep dreaming about writing a book, but they can't get the whole thing done. They join and get dropped into this badass community, write a chapter, and they are on their way!

Being able to describe your ideal client very specifically is crucial to someone else being able to connect you with the right people. There are so many questions we can ask.

Questions to Ask Your Networking Partner

Tell me about what you do.
Tell me about your ideal client.
Who do you want to be introduced to?
What's the most important thing you want me to know about what you do?
What are some of the results you get in your work?
What are your clients coming to you for?
What are they saying about the work?

These are all great questions.

I have a rather comprehensive masterclass on learning about your ideal client in The Brave Healer Resources Vault. People sell full courses about this material. It's foundational to business building and networking. When you do the ideal client work at other levels, your business becomes this magical thing that starts to attract all the people you were hoping to attract. Go do the work and keep doing it until it clicks.

Doing the work might mean you interview current clients about their needs and wants. It also might mean that you pay attention to the way you feel when you work with your clients and where the passion is. That can change. So checking in with who they are and how you feel is important. There are people I serve who I light up thinking about. I get excited. It brings me joy when I think about them and create things for them. Over the years of building my business, I've tried to ask myself why I feel that way. When I get to my why, I get to the passion that fuels everything I do. If that feeling starts to fade, I try to pay attention. Doing the ideal client work is ongoing. It's the awareness process applied to the people you serve.

Find that free masterclass here: https://lauradifranco.com/resources-vault/

This isn't one level of work, either. Every few years, I re-think my ideal client. I ask myself the question: Who is this person? Has that ideal client changed? It can shift as your business evolves.

I've got one other free resource for you in terms of questions. This is actually kind of a double-whammy resource. It's an article I wrote called *50 Things All Healers Should Write About to Promote Their Business*. If you're a content creator, writer, blogger, or email newsletter writer (and what business owners shouldn't be?), you're gonna have fun with this free resource. It is full of amazing questions you can ask your partners in networking sessions. Find the link here:

https://medium.com/@lauradifranco/50-things-all-healers-should-write-about-to-promote-their-business-a2509a3a49e1

We've talked about what questions to ask. The next most important skill is active listening. You can ask all the questions you want, but if you don't listen to the answers, you'll come up empty. I'll share some next-level info about these conversations in Part 2 also.

Chapter 4

Active Listening

Listening is an awareness practice. Most healers I know practice some kind of awareness, mindfulness, or meditation. Using awareness to listen to your networking partner is not any different. Take what you already know and apply it to listening in your conversations. Listen with your grounded, centered presence. Listen with your whole body. Feel the energy and listen to the words (and unspoken things) they're saying. This is what I think makes healers some of the best potential networkers I know—they care about the other person and want to listen.

There's a back-and-forth in a really great conversation. I'm going to share more about having those juicy conversations in Part 2 coming up. This is about asking great questions and then fully listening—full-body listening. Whole body. Breathing, grounded, centered-in-your-body awareness. This is why the energy check at the beginning of this book is so important.

Practice as you listen. Most of you healers do this all day long. It's part of who you are. So that automatically makes you an awesome networker. You just aren't connecting with what you already do really well and applying it to your business-building or networking. Use what you already know.

Listen and then take notes. I'm always taking notes during my conversations. If you and I are networking in a one-on-one, my head is looking down most of the time because I'm scribbling. And I'll usually mention it to a new person right away: "Hey, I'm taking notes, in case you were wondering."

Don't forget to take notes because you're going to want to fill those in your notebook or spreadsheet later so you can remember. I make notes and highlight, especially when they start to talk about something that helps me think of someone I want to introduce them to. The yellow highlighter is my friend during a longer, more complicated conversation when I'm in a crazy note-taking frenzy. Later, I can look back at where I want to take action. I highlight action steps.

PRACTICAL TIP: If they're talking about something important, I mirror it back. That's listening 101. Example: "You know, what I hear you saying is. . ." And then say back to them what they said. There is nothing that helps a person feel more heard than that.

When you're mirroring it back, they get excited, especially when they realize you get who they are and what they do. You will see it. They will light up. Your partner will be sitting there thinking, *Oh my gosh, they're listening. They get it.*

If you're not getting it, then ask more great questions to clarify. This is really important. If you're in a networking conversation and you're not understanding what they do or who to introduce them to, you're just not clear. You're going to do that person a favor by asking more great clarifying questions.

 **You might say:** "Hey, I'm not totally clear about what you said about that thing you do with that fire ceremony and drumming. What the heck is that?" Just be straightforward about what you don't understand. They will respect that.

When I first met my fire ceremony healer friends, I really needed to understand how they used the element of fire to release limiting beliefs. I hadn't done anything like that up until that point. I wanted to understand it so I could help talk about them and their offerings to other people I came into contact with. By the way, it's powerful medicine that fire ceremony stuff!

You can play with them a little. Please relax. A sense of humor is a good thing!

Here are some more questions about fire ceremonies or any other kind of program you don't understand:

Who is it you're serving?
Why are they coming to that ceremony (program/workshop/offering)?
What's the goal or takeaway for your clients?

Ask great questions so you can listen and get the answers, which will help you think of someone you can introduce them to.

As soon as I think of someone, I get into quick, aligned action. I make introductions during networking conversations.

 It will sound something like, "I just thought of someone I want to introduce you to. Give me just a sec, I'm going to do it right now."

Aligned action is one of the marks of a super-connector. We'll talk more about that later!

Chapter 5

Taking Aligned Action

When you think of someone you want to introduce your networking partner to, take action right away. That instantly helps establish you as a super-connector.

If I think of somebody to introduce you to, I will say, "Hey, I know this guy I'm going to introduce you to; is an email okay, or would you prefer a LinkedIn connection?" And then I'll get on it before the conversation is finished. I want to know their preferred mode of connection and try to respect that as much as possible.

As soon as I can, either right then or as soon as we click off the Zoom or the phone, I make that intro. This is not a waiting game. If you can make it happen immediately, make it happen immediately, or put it on your to-do list for later in the day, whenever you can do it. I wouldn't wait until the next day if you can help it. Why? Because you'll forget. Your notebook will be like mine, with pages of notes, and you'll lose it. So that's why I say the spreadsheet works nicely for that.

What if you can't think of anyone to introduce them to in your conversation? Make it a goal to set up a second conversation.

 **You could say,** "Hey, you know, we're at the end of our time today, and I'd really like to continue to get to know you and get a little bit clearer about what's up in your business world. Can we set up another conversation date?"

People think the magic should happen in one conversation. And while that's happened for me, sometimes it's conversation five, six, seven, eight, or nine that's the magic.

Having that unexpected follow-up conversation that turns into an introduction, referral, or collaboration is amazing. You may have just been interested in getting to know them, but then all of a sudden, you start talking about something seemingly random, there's a spark, and the conversation goes in a direction you didn't expect. You can easily find yourself in a new, unexpected business partnership or collaboration.

I want you to think about this possibility when you get tired of following up with people. You've heard, "The fortune is in the follow-up?" Well, there's a reason they say that. I would say, "Follow-up is the foundation of the fortune."

When you get tired of networking, and you will, remember what I said. I hope you email me when that happens because you're gonna be like, "Oh my gosh, if I hadn't continued the effort, that magic wouldn't have happened!" I've had it happen to me so many times now, I'm saying this to you with confidence: **Don't give up.**

Notice the people giving you that reciprocal energy, love vibe, gratitude, and generosity. Continue to follow up with the people you love talking to and feeling a high vibe from.

If it's the opposite, drop it and don't waste your time. Negative people are a no for me. I don't have time to waste with something that brings me down or otherwise squashes my purpose or vibe. Be unapologetic about it.

I know I'm explaining this to healers who understand the feeling in their body of what I'm talking about. If it's the opposite of high-vibe for you, drop it like a hot potato without guilt. Don't be afraid to rudely interrupt or let them know you have another call. Don't spend your time with people who bring you down.

Run in the other direction toward your friends who are high-vibing it. My networking friend, Mark Fujiwara, calls these people the "plus twos." The plus two conversations always leave you energized, positive, and inspired. Don't settle for less than a plus two.

PRACTICAL APPLICATION

When I ran my BETA networking course, we followed up each lesson with coaching and practical application. I thought I'd include one of our conversations here for fun so you could see how a conversation in the Brave Healer world goes down. My partner volunteer, Terri, happened to be someone who already signed up for the Brave Healer Writer's Retreat. Note: When you know you're networking with a current client, remember to respect and honor that. This conversation should be all about them.

"So Terri, I'm so happy that we set this chat up today. How's it going?"

"Life is going well. I'm a little hot here in the Texas sun, but other than that, things are going great."

"So you're actually one of my amazing people who's going to come to the retreat next year, aren't you?"

"Absolutely. I'm really excited about it. I've never been to that part of New York either, and so I'm really excited to see that part of the country. This is going to be a whole new experience for me."

"Where are you Zooming from today?"

"Fort Worth."

"Yeah. Oh wow, I'm gonna be in Fort Worth on September 20th—just a couple short weeks from now. We ought to have dinner together. I'm going to be speaking at the Badass Business Summit."

"Absolutely, we should. I know all the best safe houses if you're into that. And if not, I even know the best vegan houses."

"Terri, so you know, before we met today, I was looking to see who introduced us and want to say thank you to Ruth Souther for the introduction. How do you know Ruthie?"

"We have been bosom buddies for over a decade. We began writing together when I had a little dance studio. And we both wanted to get our stories out there. We crafted a writing circle that just grew and grew. And now we have a cooperative publishing house. We have a writing circle we call the Witch Rites Circle. We meet every week, and it's just so much fun to talk to people about pulling out their magic and making it real, getting the stories out there. What we do is help people take their stories and find clarity because it's amazing how many people have had this spiritual, magical moment. And then their words that come out are wonderful."

"Well, it sounds like we have a couple of things in common, right? That's amazing. And I've gotten to know Ruth through some retreats and writing experiences that I've had with Freedom Folk and Soul and Stephanie and Jeremy. Do you know them?"

"Yes, I do. We're going to be connecting in March. So I'll get to meet them in person for the first time. But I'm curious, have you ever worked with Ruth and her Tarot? She has this most unique style."

"Yes! She helped me after we had this amazing healing retreat together, and I got to know her and her work. We did some book publishing together with these collaborations. She actually helped me pick the date of our upcoming retreat. She did a reading for me. It was amazing. I didn't know we could choose a date based on these things. It was a really great experience working with her."

INTERMISSION

I'll pause the conversation for one moment and say that Terri and I were having a "warm" conversation. We already knew each other, and she had already purchased one of my offerings. But what if this was more of a cold-ish networking chat? How would I proceed if I didn't already know Terri?

"Terry, I know we got introduced by Ruth, and we don't know a whole lot about each other. Is it okay if I learn a bit about you and then tell you a little bit about what I'm up to? My goal would be to make an introduction for you today."

"Yeah, this is wonderful. Thank you."

I opened with that question and asked permission to get to know her. Do you see how I dropped my goal and asked for her buy-in? If you have a goal for your networking conversation, both people are clear, and you can move forward easily. Sometimes, when there's no goal, you're not really sure, and you're in there thinking, *what the heck am I doing here?* It can be really challenging.

If you don't really know this person and aren't sure what to ask, then it just starts to feel bad. The energy shifts. It turns into something that doesn't feel good or feels weird or awkward, or you don't even know what you're doing there.

 When networking, always have the goal of getting to know the person well enough that you can make an intro for them or help them solve a problem they're having.

That's it. It's that simple.

Okay, so here's how that might sound with Terri:

"So, Terri, who do you want to be introduced to this week?"

"I would love to meet some of the writers struggling with getting their story out into the world because they can't figure out how to create solid sentences around indescribable moments."

"Cool. So, do some of your services include editing? What are you doing for them?"

"What I do is I help people move beyond their blocks in their writing or to take their story up a level. It's a lot of brainstorming and interaction and really diving into the emotional connection the writer wants their reader to have with their words. So I bring clarity to them on that. So a bit more of a book coach or writing coach in that respect."

"Do you have separate editing services aside from that?"

"It's kind of a combination, depending on the story. If they're writing, let's say, a 3000-word story for a publication, then it's all of that. If they're writing a book, then it's more of an either-or."

"Okay, so I'm hearing that it depends on what exactly they're writing. Do you have a favorite introduction? Would you want that intro of the essay writer, or would you want the person who's writing their whole book?"

INTERMISSION

So, readers, I tried to get clear in that last piece. This was me asking clarifying questions. Because I don't yet have someone in mind, right? And Terri and I have a lot in common. We do similar things. I want to make sure I'm introducing the perfect person to her.

There's also this thought in my head, and I'm gonna call this out so that none of you have to feel weird in your own conversations about it. She already told me they publish. And I'm a publisher. Am I thinking *competition*? No. I'm thinking: *How can I collaborate with her?*

Because if they're publishing solo books (which I don't do too many of), I'm an expert at the collaborative community-promoted launch. The question becomes about how I can get information from Terri to know who this perfect introduction is. And at the same time, I hope she asks me, too. We could be excellent referral partners for each other.

If you start to chat with somebody, sometimes that funky competitive brain of yours starts in: *Oh, they do what I do. Why am I talking to this person? Why would I even be networking with someone who gives the exact same service?* Pause yourself if this happens because you don't know yet. Shift your energy immediately. Shift to: *What else is possible here?*

And, the truth is, I don't know yet. It's my job to keep asking until something clicks or not.

Learning how to talk about yourself in a way that helps you get introductions is a skill. You're going to have to pick one ideal client for the conversation you're in that day, the mood you're in, and the energy you're in. If you can't get them clear, you lose.

If you *can* get them clear, you win, and you could possibly win an intro that could be a client or a total business-changing partner. Think collaboration over competition, and you'll win every time.

PRACTICAL TIP: If you're networking with someone who has similar services, find the service they provide that you don't (and that you don't want to provide) and bring them in to help your audience with a special workshop. Do that for each other. The introduction and referral potential is unlimited.

Do you see the win here? It could be a really big one for both of us.

The main point I want you to take away from this chapter is the aligned actions you can take, either in the moment or right after the call, to connect your networking partner. Whether you're making an introduction for them, helping them find a resource for a problem they're having, or setting them up with a podcast interview, the objective is to act as soon as you can and when it's appropriate.

Examples – Getting to Know Your Passions / Sharing Mine

Here are a couple of examples of how getting to know those I connect with—understanding their passions and helping them to understand mine—has helped me make intros for them and helped grow my business.

I sit on the board of directors of The Inkwell, founded by Dinahsta "Miss Kiane" Thomas. She's a poet here in the D.C. area. The Inkwell serves troubled youth through therapeutic writing programs. This was a no-brainer for me to serve with her because of my passion for using writing as a healing tool. I can talk about it, and I can talk about what she does with passion. I understand her "why." I had so many questions about what she does and an interest in getting to know her and her company at another level. The collaboration potential was palpable!

One of my huge business goals and passions is to be able to write $10,000 checks to the charities I love. So, I partner with nonprofits. If I'm writing $10,000 checks to charity, that's a whole other level. It's a huge goal of mine, and I'm excited about the energy of generosity and gratitude. It's a huge manifesting energy. Obviously, I have to be making enough money to be that generous.

Sitting on a board was a new activity for me. It was a new, other-level networking move. And it has been amazing. I've met new people who've become powerful connections, attended events and sponsored events, and have been able to get myself and my company out there in a bigger way as a result.

Here's another example: I'm hosting an exciting writer's retreat in Upstate New York in May of 2024, and I'm partnering with a couple of organizations to give back chunks of my profit to help those in need of authentic healing programs. I want to be able to offer scholarships to these programs because I know how important authentic healing is to individuals who've undergone trauma.

I want to partner with people who dedicate their lives to helping people heal and recover from trauma. My first 30-year career was just this. I'm a retired holistic physical therapist. Authentic healing matters to me. It's what helped me live an extraordinary life. Partnering with people I trust who provide these powerful and profound experiences to others is another no-brainer. It's a huge ripple for me. It's my legacy.

Partnering with people like Stephanie Urbina Jones and Jeremy Pajer of Freedom, Folk, and Soul has been an incredible experience. We're coming together with a common mission and goal, and when we come together, we're able to create something much bigger than if we tried to do it on our own.

In Part 2, I'll get into more fun ways to have positive, productive, business-building conversations—the juicy ones!

Part 2

The Art of Juicy Conversations

I remember talking to Donnie Boivin one of the first times we met and wishing I'd scheduled more than an hour because the get-to-know-you phase quickly turned into some powerful collaborative energy.

"We should teach a class together," I suggested.

"Let's do it!"

And we were off to the races, creating and implementing together. What made those first conversations great for me was that we shared a similar sense of humor. Each took responsibility for bringing our own energy and resources to the table and seemed to have very common goals and struggles. We are both great question-askers and were genuinely interested and curious about each other's businesses, lives, and dreams.

When someone cares, the conversation can go deep fast. When someone is authentic and isn't trying to be someone they're not, trust is built quickly, and what follows is friendship.

I remember Donnie saying to our group one day, "Don't invest time with someone you wouldn't hang out with otherwise. You have to truly like people."

Some of us are better at conversation than others. It took me a long time to have a desire to get better at having conversations with people and to truly want to get to know them. Once that genuine curiosity, desire, and caring were in place, the rest was about practicing some general techniques that, like any skill, get better with time.

Chapter 6

How to Start a Great Conversation

Take a deep breath and bask in the gratitude of all the beautiful people all over the world who have an interest in building awesome relationships with you. *That* is how to start a juicy conversation.

Start with energy and intention.

It's never too late to meet a business partner who changes your entire business trajectory. When people bring energy, enthusiasm, and passion to conversations, I feel so grateful.

Whatever stage you're at on this journey—even not liking it so much but knowing you really want to do more and get better at it—all the way to knowing it could build your empire—this is what we're doing! That is how cool this is. Feel that energy right now with a couple of deep breaths. This is what we're here to do. We want to get to know each other so we can make awesome introductions, build relationships, build our businesses, and leave our legacies in a bigger way.

It's big potatoes stuff. So start by getting into the feels of that!

The most common feeling people share about networking is their dislike or fear. They aren't sure about what to say, who to be, or what to do. They're nervous going in.

Newsflash: it's not about you! Check that energy and mindset as you begin conversations or in between conversations. What else is possible?

I set my energy for everything I do as much as possible. When I remember to set my energy and intention for everything I do, those moments tend to be pretty amazing. When I forget, or I'm tired, or rushing and hopping to the next thing, and don't have time to do that, guess what happens? It goes south pretty fast. As soon as your energy turns in a bad direction, it can drag everything down with it.

Flip your switch and aim the energy and intention at your partner. Ask yourself some better questions to set the stage for success:

How can I take responsibility for getting to know this person well enough that I can make a really cool introduction for them today?

Then, all of a sudden, this whole fear about talking about ourselves will dissolve.

Maybe you've been thinking: *I don't know how to sell my stuff. I don't know how to network.* Stop thinking that way. All of that stuff is going to come with practice. With awareness, you have a choice. This starts with awareness and mindset.

And yes, there's the art of sales conversations—networking 102 and 103: How do you disqualify a client? There are layers of skills. The first step is getting comfortable asking great questions and getting to know your friends and business partners.

If you have that good energy, you're 75 percent there already. Now it's about how to ask those great questions and develop some know-love-trust relationships with your colleagues.

Get clear on what your partner does. Get clear on their ideal client. We're always getting clear on our own, but what about their ideal client? Find the passion in them. Get to the question that lights them up, where they sit up a little taller, and they start to talk louder. You'll see they're getting excited. That's the place to go after in your juicy conversations.

I shared some info about what questions to ask and about how to listen actively. Aside from asking great questions, active listening is so important. I also shared about taking aligned action that really establishes you as a connector.

During a conversation, I've got my notebook, and I'm writing notes as they're talking as I clue into who I might introduce to them. I write that as a little to-do list in my notebook during the conversation. I write it down and take action the minute I get off the call with them or even during the call. And, yes, I'm repeating this bit about taking action in hopes that you're paying attention to the fact that **action makes you a super-connector.**

Now, more about the art of juicy conversations.

What Kind of Conversation is It?

It could be a cold introduction, a warm introduction, or a little hotter introduction, depending on how well you know the person or don't. For each of those scenarios, there might be a different way to open up the conversation, depending on if you know the person already or not.

Some conversations are "cold," meaning it's a get-to-know-the-person call. I go in with an open mind to see what I can learn. Some cold conversations have turned into business partnerships!

Keep your mind open. You may find something in common and start to talk about this or that, and you never know. One thing I love so much in a cold conversation is when I can make an introduction that makes a difference in the person's life. That awesome energy I get to feel is something I bring to myself as well when I curate my mindset.

Y'all can feel the energy behind what you're doing here, right? When you constantly get to feel that way because of the connections you made, you automatically get to live in that higher vibe energy first and foremost, but then guess what you attract more of? More of that same awesome energy!

I always make connections without the expectation that that same person is going to make an intro back to me. Who knows? So, I let go of that expectation, detach, and I keep connecting. And believe me, people connect people to me in reciprocation. It may not be the same person who reciprocates that energy, but it comes back to me. I love that.

What Happens When the Conversation Isn't Juicy?

What happens when you have a conversation with someone who needs to get better at talking about themselves in a really clear way so that you know what they do? When you're in it, and there's a lot of awkward energy, and your partner is droning on about every little detail, but meanwhile, you're still very unclear, what do you do?

The exercise I like to share in this situation is this: If you were going to say what you do in 10 or 15 seconds or three to five words—so simple that a fifth grader could understand it—what would that sound like?

Example: I publish books for healers.

Come up with a short, sweet version like this for your business that's so clear a fifth-grader can understand it. Then, let the conversation flow from there. Allow your partner to ask questions. Don't fill in all the blanks right away. See what questions they ask.

You need a starting point that makes sense to somebody to spur some questions. But if it's too detailed, you'll confuse and overwhelm people. I take responsibility for this and start my question-asking if I'm not clear, but sometimes I have to actually pause people and say, "Hey, this isn't clear to me yet. Is there another way you can describe this?"

Sometimes, you just have to be in their face a little with the next question that tells them, "Sorry, you're not doing a great job of this. I need it to be different for me." We all have different filters for how we receive and hear information. And they will be grateful that you stopped them to get clear. Most people don't press the question because they're afraid of offending the person, so they sit there, unclear, and get to the end of a conversation without clarity and without any ideas for an introduction. That's a bummer.

What if It's Just Not Working?

Sometimes, it just isn't working out. Sometimes, it's not a match, or maybe it's just not working out energy-wise or information-wise, and you need to say, "Next!" That's okay. If you're pouring in your energy and effort, and it's not being reciprocated, or it's just not working out, you may need to shut that down because it starts to feel draining. Not every conversation I have is a miracle. Some of them really suck.

Live and learn, move on, and you'll be better for the next one. You very quickly learn who you want to have more conversations with, and you get a little bit choosier about reaching out.

Get more purposeful and choosy about who you're gonna spend your time and efforts with. Test it out, learn all the lessons, and practice. That's how I did it.

One thing I really loved on my learning journey about networking (from people who were great at it) was hearing their ideas for scripts or ways to talk to people.

Below are some ways to open things up. Choose one that feels good, and go out there and try it out!

Gratitude

First and foremost, **I open with** gratitude on purpose. And no matter how rushed or stressed or tired I am, I'll get into the conversation and start with, "Whoa, thank you so much for meeting with me today." Because they're taking precious time out of their day to be with me.

That shifts me automatically. Gratitude does that! And you all know that. It's a tool and strategy we use for our lives, so how about with every networking conversation? It's the same energy and even more important, in my opinion, because your business is world-changing, legacy-leaving work. It's the part of your life that moves the good stuff out into the world in a bigger way.

"Thank you so much for meeting with me. I can't wait to get to know you."

Curiosity

The next best way to open is with curiosity about them and what they do. Genuine curiosity builds trust. You must couple the questions with active listening for them to feel genuine.

I say: "Tell me a little bit about your interests." Not a question but a great, open-ended way to start a conversation.

"Tell me about yourself and your business."

"What matters to you right now?"

Just a simple question, right? But it's a powerful one that helps the person focus on passion.

"What inspired you to reach out today?" Or, "How did you find me?" That's a good one for a 'cold call'. I also always ask, if I don't already know, how the person found me to make sure I know how these amazing conversations are getting booked.

Do Your Research

Before you hop on a call, do some research, even if it's five minutes of stalking their LinkedIn profile. Go in with something about what you've read there. Anything will do. It shows you took the time to look at it. This builds trust. Do the research about who or how you were connected ahead of time, and that becomes a great opener.

 I might say: "I'm so happy that (name) introduced us. How do you know (name)?"

 **You'll often hear me opening with:** "I'm so happy to talk to you today; I can't wait to learn more about you. Tell me everything!" And that always gets a laugh because we both know we don't have enough time for the whole life or business story, but it breaks the ice a little.

 **Here's another way to say it:** "I saw that you're a (fill in the blank) from your LinkedIn profile. Tell me more.

Do you know what that does for the person? They sit up taller and pay attention because you did your research. Now they know you're a person who cared enough to take five minutes.

Could be LinkedIn, could be their website, or Facebook, whatever. You read enough to find something out about the person, and now you're going in, and you're not cold anymore.

Note: I don't always have time to research, and that's okay, too. Do it when you can.

I got on one call, and we were both in the same situation. We were both Zoom hopping that day, one call to the next. Within the first 60 seconds, we both admitted that to each other—that we didn't have time and were both searching for the contact and couldn't find it and didn't have time to look at each other's information. It's totally okay to call yourself out because *that* can be the icebreaker. **It's just you being real. And real people like real people.**

That moment was the bonding moment. And because we were each pretty cool people with a sense of humor, we just laughed about it and started there.

 **You could say,** "Normally, I have a minute to read all about you, but I couldn't do that before our session today. Tell me about yourself." It's okay to use that as your opener with a genuine interest in getting to know them.

That's a cold connection, but what about a warm one?

A Warm Opener

How are you starting the conversation in a situation where it's warm? Maybe you already know it's a sales call, or the person flat-out told you they want info about what you offer. Maybe it was a referral, not an introduction. We could have a whole class on this alone. And, in fact, there's a whole chapter later about this!

When you're networking, know who you're talking to and what kind of conversation it is. And then you can decide how you're opening up. Cold, warm, or hot, it's really great to go in ready with the info, energy, intention, and goals that serve both parties.

If it's somebody who's really busy, who's giving you 15 or 20 minutes of their time, you're not going to talk about the weather for ten minutes. Read the room. Understand they probably have to get down to business quickly.

Some Warm Opener Ideas

"What's new in your world?" I love asking my friends who I already know this question because I truly want to know what's new! I sometimes even use it for a cold opener. And then they laugh because we don't know each other. It's just like a friend, "Hey, what's new? Tell me everything."

 Another option is, "What's something interesting about you that I don't know yet? I love that one. Depending on the conversation, you could use this at any time.

 Here's one I really love: "What are you most excited about in your business?"

 Or, "What aspect of your business are you growing?"

We're getting a little bit more honed in on business now, and you can move into that as soon as you're comfortable because most people who signed up for a networking call are interested in talking about business.

 **Another option:** "What has been bringing you joy lately?"

Try different things. See what sparks the best conversations and why. Experiment. Don't be afraid to change it up!

If you're someone (like me) who doesn't like the superficial chit-chat, then open with something more personal and/or business-related. You can open with, "Thanks so much for meeting with me today. What do I need to know about (fill in the blank with what that referral was about)." Just get to it. Gauge it, try it out, and see how it works, depending on the kind of introduction that was made and the kind of person you're chatting with.

The next thing to ponder is the listening-talking dance. Some mentors of mine talk about the 80/20 rule (listen 80% of the time and talk 20%), but I think that this is always a dance that can change from moment to moment. I agree that we should aim to listen more than speak, and I also think that it depends on what kind of conversation you're having, how well you know each other, and what the goals of the conversation are.

Ready to dance?

Chapter 7

The Listening—Talking Dance

How do we master this listening—talking dance? I don't like the formulas that have been shared with me because it just gives you something else to worry about when you're trying to have this juicy conversation. More of a balance might be something to go for. Make sure you're experiencing both listening and speaking.

If you talk the entire time, you're not giving the person a chance to talk. You're not pausing. Don't do that. Sometimes, when I'm nervous, I do that. That awareness helps. You have to have some self-awareness in a conversation. I've actually called myself out when I'm nervous and said, "Oh my gosh, I'm talking too much. I must be nervous. Tell me about you." Just be real, people. Your networking partners will respect your authenticity.

Do that—say it, and be vulnerable. Put it out there when you catch yourself. We all do it. They'll chuckle, and they'll be fine. In fact, they will appreciate you for that awareness.

If you have 20 minutes with somebody who could change your business life and they have advice, support, an introduction, or something to tell you, and you know it, speak for a moment and then remember to shut up and let them teach you. As I said earlier, the listening-talking dance is more related to the circumstances of the conversation.

If you were going into this conversation knowing you were about to meet (for free) with the most successful business coach on the planet, would you talk for 15 minutes? No, (I hope) you would not.

 You would say, "Hey, I'm so grateful to be meeting with you today. I'm Laura. I publish books for healers. How can I support what you're doing in the world?"

And I would shut the hell up and let that person drive the rocket ship because they're going to ask me questions to get to know what they need to know about me. And then, who knows what golden nugget they're gonna drop? Maybe they came into the conversation already having an introduction for me or what they wanted to know. Meanwhile, here I was, filling up all the space with my chatter because I was nervous, and it's 18 minutes in, and they have a meeting in two minutes. Don't do that, brave healers.

Know who you're talking to and balance your talking and listening. But if you weigh heavier toward one or the other, lean toward listening. Ask great questions, pause, and listen. Ask another great question and pause. Always break it up with pauses to see if there's something your partner needs or wants to say. Don't miss that chance to hear from them.

When it comes to formulas, do what's right for you and what's working. Read the room. Be flexible. Be aware. Be generous.

One note about not talking. Yes, I said *not* talking. What I've noticed in some meetings with experienced networkers is because they're trying so hard to follow the 80-20 rule, they aren't talking at all. OMG people. That's not how it works either! I'm here to get to know you, too. If you hold back, then I start to wonder why. If you don't share about yourself, it's a problem. Another way to understand this is if you don't give me an opportunity to know you, you're being selfish and also not contributing to the dance. It takes two: back and forth, ebb and flow, listen and talk.

The only real rule I like to follow is to have fun.

I measure my success in life (and conversations) by how much fun I'm having. Hopefully, that means they are having fun, too. Knowing what to say is part intuitive and part practice. It does help to understand how to carry forward (or close) a conversation. I'll cover different kinds of conversations and how to navigate them next.

Chapter 8

How to Know What to Say

More on Different Kinds of Conversations

If it's a get-to-know-you chat, then that's a particular kind of conversation. I talked about all the ways we could open up that conversation earlier. I'm trying to get to know the person. I don't know what's in store for this possible collaboration or relationship. I just really have to get into the conversation and get to know them.

They might want information about what you do. That's a different kind of conversation. It's a little bit of a get-to-know-you, but then you can move into the topic the person scheduled the meeting about and answer any questions they have.

 In my world, **it might sound like,** "I know you scheduled this session to pick my brain about publishing. How can I help?"

My goal is to give them as much value in our time together as possible. I will coach in those sessions to help get them on the right track. I try to keep the time to what we agreed upon and not over-give. When you do that, the energy exchange feels off-balance and not good. But even in these circumstances (they have questions and want info), I try to pause and ask great questions. I want them to talk as much as I do! I still want to be a great listener. I want that dance to happen. This kind of conversation is leaning a bit more toward a sales conversation because they already inquired about your services.

What to Do if They Won't Stop Talking

I get this question a lot. What do you do if they won't stop talking? You might have a 30-minute conversation booked, and it is literally 23 minutes in, and they haven't asked you one question about yourself. You kind of get the idea of what's happening here. Even after ten straight minutes—think about that for a minute—you have some feelings about it. What's your boundary here? If that's happening to you, how many minutes does it take to intuitively know what's happening and change course?

This does take some practice and many conversations to realize when someone is doing this and doesn't really plan on a two-way conversation. They may be a bit unconscious about what they're doing, but either way, you're going to need to intervene, and sometimes it's going to feel like a rude interruption.

If it's clear they're not going to give you room (the clock is ticking, and it's obvious) and they're not going to be asking any questions, it's not going to be reciprocal. Check in with yourself. What's your plan? As you have these different conversations and experiences, you're for sure going to understand better and better. So you've got to keep having them.

I changed my available networking time slots from 45 minutes to 25 minutes because of this. My Acuity scheduling link (the scheduling system I use) has a 25-minute networking chat option. I call that session a "Connection and Clarity" session. We connect, get to know each other, and get clarity about what each other does and how to support.

I made them 25 minutes so that people understand that this is going to be a dance back and forth. If they want my expertise about publishing or books, that's cool. But if they talk the whole time, they're not going to give me a chance to give them what they want.

 If half of that time is taken up, it's going to be one of those, and at the end, **I'm going to have to say**, "Oh, you know, gosh, it was great to get to know you and your situation. We're running up against the time here today. What's the best step forward

for you?" Decide what you're going to say when this happens and how to move forward.

I wrote a blog about interrupting people because there's a time and a place for it when you don't want to waste your time, and you want to have great conversations, and you realize what's happening. There are some really great ways to gently interrupt if you have to. You'll find that info in Part 5.

I know that's tough for some of you because you're great listeners and don't want to interrupt people. You're healers. You're holding that healing space for somebody else. But heck, this is a networking conversation. Understand where you're over-giving, stand up tall inside your own worthiness, and set those boundaries. Sometimes, you do have to interrupt people, and that's okay.

The next skill is the close. And getting closure in a conversation is important. It will truly be the way you build your relationship further or not.

Let's get to it!

Chapter 9

How to Effectively Close a Conversation

Whether you're interrupting to close, you're just closing because it's approaching the end of the chat time, or you're actually closing by making a decision about a sale or a collaboration, there are great ways to close a conversation to make it a productive, positive experience with a possible great outcome for both parties.

How would you close a conversation in the most effective magical way? In the case of the clock, I know I've got this 25 minutes, and we're headed to 20, then 23. We can see the clock. It's time to acknowledge that and wrap it up.

Know where you're at in a conversation. Watch the time. Be a great timekeeper in networking conversations. If the person's schedule was for 25 minutes, honor it. Pause at 20 or 23 minutes, and **you can say**, "Hey, I know we only have a few minutes left. Is there anything else you want to talk about today?"

Closing could also sound like, "Hey, this has been such a great conversation. I realized we just have a few minutes left. Would you be interested in scheduling a follow-up?" That's one I use a lot if neither of us has extra time, but it was just getting good, and there's still a list of things to chat about.

When it's a great conversation, and I have ten more questions for them, and I'm also trying to honor the time, great, then it's time to book conversation number two.

You might say: "Let's get it on the books right now before we stop," is what I'll say. That's a perfect way to close because you don't leave the scheduling for later. But if you end that conversation without taking that scheduling action, make sure you do it immediately or as soon as you think of it. Don't forget! Send them the email before you move on to something else: "Thank you so much for chatting today. Here's my link. Let's get something booked for next week or two weeks from now."

This is great, especially when you didn't quite get to the place you wanted to get in terms of talking about each other's businesses or work, or you wanted to know more about what they did, but it was kind of a get-to-know-you instead.

Bottom line: It all depends.

If it's a little bit warmer, it can be more of a sales conversation—they had interest in your services, and they've been asking you about it the whole conversation. If you're getting to the end of the time, it's the same thing: honor the time, look up at that clock, and say, "Hey, I see we have just a few minutes left. Are there any questions you had about book publishing that I haven't answered for you today? Are you interested in having the link to my program?" Fill in the blanks with your services.

And that gets me to when you're closing with a call to action for the sale. This may be the most challenging piece for you but don't despair. This is all about practice and detaching from the outcome. **You're not selling; you're sharing with passion.**

Sales Closure

Get some closure on what that next action step is going to be if it's a sales conversation or happens to turn into one. A sales conversation is more about interest in your services, and now you're sitting there wondering if they're going to actually sign up, and there's some conversation back and forth, and the person's response is, "I'm going to think about it a bit, and I'll get back to you."

You've all had that scenario. It's very difficult if you leave a conversation without a clear step forward. Do not end the conversation with them saying, "I'll think about it and get back to you."

What I'd come back with would be something like, "Okay, thank you so much for considering it. I'm going to assume this is a no for now unless I hear from you."

What happens if you haven't set a deadline is that they aren't going to get back to you in a certain time, and you'll go crazy. You don't know if you should follow up. You don't know how often you should follow up. You don't know what they're thinking. Oh my gosh, what a mess. Get some closure before you hop off the call.

 **You might say,** "Hey, I realize you want to think about it a little bit. That's totally cool. If I don't hear from you within a week, I'll assume this is a no, but in the meantime, if you have any questions for me or if I can help clarify anything, please reach out."

If you wanted to follow up at the end of those seven days, you could send a quick email, but don't be surprised if you don't get a reply.

Closure on the call is a beautiful feeling in all cases, especially if it's a sales call. You won't have to sit around waiting and wondering. You can just move on to your next conversation.

Setting up that second conversation date is a great solution for closure as well.

 **You might say,** "I understand you want to think about it. How about we get back on a call on Friday so I can answer any remaining questions you might have?" Set a date for conversation number two so you can have closure. If you make the date and they cancel it, it was a no, Y'all. Just go with your intuition here. And don't sit around waiting and torturing yourself about trying to hear back from them. Take control of that. Let go and move on.

See Part 4 for more on the sales conversation. It's an art and skill all by itself.

The next chapter has more scripts, so you have ideas going into your conversations and can practice. See which resonates the most.

Chapter 10

Scripts and Practice

We have to practice to get better at this networking thing. I may have mentioned that once or twice so far, right? We must practice the sales conversations, asking for the sale, and verbalizing all this stuff. This gets so much better (natural and authentic feeling) with practice. In the beginning, it feels stiff and awkward because you aren't used to it. That's normal!

What helps is to read and hear examples and then find what resonates and model that.

EXAMPLE: Here's an example sales call to action for my business that I'd share when someone has asked to "pick my brain" about self-publishing and we're coming to the end of the call: "Hey, I've been teaching you all about this self-publishing process in this half hour. Can I send you our self-publishing coaching package information?"

There are so many versions of ways you can ask for the sale or at least move toward the next step.

If I get a "No, I'm not really interested" or "No, I don't think I'm ready for that," fine. I've got my answer. I'm not going to spend more energy trying to talk them into a yes.

Ask for the sale and detach from the outcome of the reply.

"Are you interested in this program?" "Do you want one of the spots that are left?" Don't be afraid to ask.

One great way to ask for the sale is to include permission to say no.

 You might say: "Hey, it's totally okay if this is a no. But if you're ready to join the program, I'd love to send you the info!" In this case, you've given them permission to say no, and there's much less pressure and stress in the conversation.

Do you see what I did there with that little pre-sentence? "It's totally fine if this is a no today." And then you must detach. This energy and mindset frees them up a little and feels better for you, too. They may have questions; they may have hesitations—just detach but get closure.

A really nice way to end most of these conversations and get a little closure is, "Who can I introduce you to right now?" That's the "give" in the conversation I always remember to offer. Always ask, "Who are you looking to be introduced to right now?" Or, "How can I help you?" When you make sure to make this about them, even when it's a sales conversation, you build that know-love-trust relationship even further.

Finding the Words for Different Scenarios

What I've learned from my practice is that each conversation is so different, and I try not to assume or guess what kind it's going to be until I'm in it and find out. I like to start each one with the "get-to-know-you" attitude, whether it's a sales conversation or not because even if they want what I'm offering, it's the relationship that's going to create the magic moving forward. What's the magic? Maybe an intro or referral from that person.

I'm a get-to-it kind of girl, and in my networking conversations, I want to get to an outcome, and I'm a little impatient when it comes to that, I admit. Many people you talk to will be very busy people who want to make sure they're making great connections but also not wanting to waste time.

If it's is a warm conversation, and I know the person and what they're up to, I'll go right in and say, "What do you need help with?" But if they just keep explaining different things and haven't answered me, I'm just going to keep wrangling them back in so I can get to the helping. That's my personality, and I have to learn to listen a bit more sometimes. You'll get to know yourself in networking. You'll be able to feel your triggers, impatience, and when you need to check in on your own energy.

If someone's been in my world multiple times as a client, I'm usually not going to ask them to sign up for anything else I have going on. I'm here to fully serve and help at another level. I will always say, "Thank you so much for being my client and for being in my world. How can I help you today?"

 My friend and colleague, Donnie, dropped an important nugget for me recently in our networking endeavors with Success Champion Networking: **"Your referrals will come from your clients. Introductions can come from anybody."**

Referrals will come from those people you already serve. They might refer somebody because you've been working together for a while and built a relationship, friendship, and trust. Most of you healers work off of word-of-mouth referrals. You understand this. What you don't understand is the introductions, how and when to make those, and who they might come from.

If you get out of your head that everybody should be making the referrals and know it's your clients who will refer, but that everyone else is about intros and getting to know them at the next level, oh my gosh, this will take all the pressure off your conversations. You'll just want to keep having more conversations.

We should all want more intros!

How Did You Find Me?

Remember to ask people how you were connected—really important. If you don't know somebody or how you were connected, that'll be the first question, and it's a great icebreaker.

You might ask: "How do we know each other?" Or, "I'm so glad to chat with you today. Remind me how we were connected?" This is if you don't already know, which does happen. That's a great way to start when it's a cold conversation, and you can't remember who connected you.

What would be even more awesome is **this version:** "I see we were connected by Bob Smith. How do you know Bob?" In that case, I made sure to go look up who connected us before the conversation started, and I was ready with that question. And then I'll follow it with, "I want to hear everything about what you do, what's going on in your world?" Or I'll ask something similar to get the conversation going.

When They Bring Up Something That's in Your Wheelhouse

When I have a conversation with someone who I don't know and am getting to know, and they voluntarily bring up something that has to do with what I do, what a fun gift that is. In my case, that's when they tell me they have a book or are thinking about writing a book.

I have to laugh about how many cold conversations I go into, and they never tell me they wrote a book, or they end up telling me in minute 23 of a 25-minute conversation. But I love it because that's a perfect chance to say, "Oh, wow, I want to hear everything about that. Let's schedule a follow-up!"

If they mention it with plenty of time, I'm super happy to let them know what my expertise is and offer my knowledge or advice, but I always try to ask permission first.

I might ask: "Oh, wow, how exciting! Well, I'm a publisher! I'm so happy to hear you wrote a book. Is there anything you need help with?" Or, "I'm so happy you're thinking about writing a book. I happen to be a publisher! Would you like me to share some starting points with you?"

It's nice to ask before you start to coach or share. And if you do, always remember to shut up and let them talk, too.

When a Cold Conversation Turns Warm Very Quickly

If I realize someone is going from cold to warm, meaning we figure out what each other does, and there's an instant synergy and interest in knowing more about the service, then we can shift the conversation into a sales conversation as quickly as we feel like, with an energy of generosity. To me, that means that if I learn someone wants to know more about my book publishing services or programs, I'll make sure to give them lots of quality info, coaching, next steps, etc., and then close with the invite to send them more information. It's more of a "giving value" session than me trying to sell them.

When you realize someone is your perfect ideal client on a cold networking call, it can be tempting to try to sell. I'm very guilty of this because I get so excited about being able to help them with what I was born to do. The conversation can turn warm really fast. So, I have to remember that I want to know how I can serve her at the next level.

 I might ask: "Are you okay with me giving you a couple of suggestions right now?"

Who would say no to that, right? I'm a giver in this way and really want them to feel like they have someone who cares about their project and can be a resource for them moving forward.

When the conversation turns warm, and I realize I can give information the person really wants and needs, I'll go there, but one thing you heard me do was ask for permission first because I tend to over-give and overwhelm people with my book advice. Most healers are overgivers. Know this about yourself in networking conversations. Reign it in a little. It isn't always effective.

 I might ask: "Is it okay if I give you a couple of tips right now?" This is just another version of the one above. And even if they say yes, which they always do, I have to be very mindful to slow down and pause to ask if they have questions. When you turn on a firehose, nobody wins there. You just feel soaked and overwhelmed and have a deep desire to go home and dry off.

The other problem with overgiving is burnout and an unfair energy exchange. Limiting networking calls to a certain time is part of the solution.

You can always close with a call to action for your coaching services. **Mine would sound something like:** "I know we're at the end of our time today, and it sounds like you have a lot of questions. I have a coaching service if you think a session would help you move forward. Would you like more details about that?" And if they say yes, you can tell them your fees and set something up or give them your scheduling link.

Because the other scenario that happens, aside from you over-giving, is them over-taking. And if you haven't set boundaries on your call times, and the person wants that advice and coaching and just keeps asking, you may begin to feel that energy shift negatively. Healers, always check your energy and, more importantly, set your free networking or discovery calls with a time boundary that feels great to you.

It's so important to be straightforward and clear with people. That builds transparency and respect. When you're clear, people appreciate it. There's no questioning. And they can opt in for more or not. There's no wishy-washiness. There's no weird feeling. If you're straightforward with that conversation, it's going to be fun. And you'll be able to share about what you have going on, and everybody's going to feel pretty good about it.

Rejection and Detachment

In our conversation scenarios, I often have people asking about what to do with that rejection feeling. I say, "Detach from the outcome." This is a mindset and energetic activity.

Go in with a mindset of curiosity, to get to know them, and not to sell your stuff. When you go in that way, there's no rejection. When you go in with the energy to serve them, there's no rejection.

Detach energetically and mentally from an outcome. Truth is, you don't know what the outcome will be. So don't hope or expect anything. Start with the genuine desire to get to know the other person and serve them the best you can. Even if you think this was supposed to be a sales conversation, don't assume. You're still moving into it with the energy of service and gratitude. I always ask, "How can I help?"

It's so great to remember these golden nuggets when you get a "no":

A no might be the Universe protecting you.

A no might be the Universe setting you up for something better.

A no might be a "not right now."

A no is never personal.

A no frees you up to move forward to the next conversation.

Disqualifying

Disqualifying a prospective client is Networking 102. But I'm going to give you a taste of it now because it's the most freeing, amazing feeling to have the confidence to disqualify someone.

This isn't a negative thing. You're doing them and you a favor. You're cutting out all the bullshit and making it easy on both of you by asking questions that help you get clear about whether or not this person is the right client for you and you are right for them.

That's what you're doing when you disqualify someone. It's about asking them very specific questions so that when you hear the answers, you know exactly if this person fits in your "ideal client" lane or not.

To get to the skill level where you can disqualify someone, you must understand exactly who you're looking for and come up with a set of questions to ask that helps you know they fit into your criteria. All of a sudden, this isn't about them saying yes or no. It's about you making sure they are a perfect fit for you and what you're offering. This totally changes the game of sales. It shifts that super-icky feeling of trying to sell them something into taking control of who you want to serve.

You take your power back when you learn how to disqualify someone. The energy shifts, and it's healthier. And you help the other person because there's no forcing or talking someone out of their objections. Ugh, don't get me started on that.

When you disqualify, you just keep getting to the no, and you do it quickly, so there's no waste of time.

Last Word About the No

So they say no. You have your clear answer, and you can move forward to closing the call. But here's what I don't want you to forget to say.

 You might say: "Thank you so much for your time today. Maybe you know somebody who this would be perfect for? Please keep me in mind. I'd be so grateful for the referral."

Your person might be a no, but be brave about asking them to think of someone they know to introduce to you.

I had a call with someone and shared about our writers' retreat, and it was an example of a no. Here's how that went down:

"Thanks for letting me tell you about the retreat, Nicole. I'm really excited about it. I get that it's a no for you. All good. If you happen to know anyone in upstate New York, we're going to have this at the Honors Haven Retreat Center, and, who knows, you might know some people up there who might want to come to write for these two books I'm doing, and it would be easy for them to attend. Please keep me in mind if you think of anyone!"

Her response: "Absolutely! I'd be happy to!"

If you've been your authentic, badass, awesome self, even when people say no, they do want to help you.

Another Powerful Way to Share

When you're starting out in this networking game and in practice mode, a really genuine way to practice your call to action, whether or not you really know if the person is perfect for it or not, is to just tell people you're practicing and ask if you can try it out on them.

I honestly love saying something like: "This will be one of the first times I'm sharing this info with someone. Would you mind if I tried out my call to action for this program on you? I'd love the feedback."

This is so brave because it's going to feel so uncomfortable to you. You're going to feel vulnerable. But it's badass because you're just being real, and they'll feel like they're helping you, whether they are a yes, a no, or can eventually refer someone to you.

Should you ask why someone is a no?

Some people want to know why someone is a no. I don't really need to know why, but if you do, beware. Most of the time, the reason you're asking is because you're afraid it's personal. And you'll get yourself into some self-sabotaging if you go there. So check yourself if you're asking why.

If you really want to know, then you can be brave about it. But otherwise, taking it personally is a mistake. It's not about you.

I think I'm going to have this put on my gravestone: *She learned how to not take anything personally.* That will truly be a win in life.

What to Do With a Fake Yes

What the heck is a fake yes? It's when someone, out of discomfort or fear, says, "Yes, I'd like to sign up for that; send me the link," and actually never wanted to or meant to say yes but was too uncomfortable to say no.

The problem is, when you close the call and send them the info, you're never going to hear from them again. What I suggest in this instance (they say yes, you send the info, and then get ghosted) is that you follow up one time, and if you don't hear back, your next follow-up says, "Hi Bob, just following up on your request for the link and information. If I don't hear back by (Fill in a date/deadline), I'll assume this is a no for you. I'm always here for questions."

What this does for you is help you not be waiting around for an answer and dangling in the "I don't know what to do" zone for too long. Take your power back and just be clear about it. Get closure.

Guess what happens, then? You open your energetic field for a new person to walk into your world. You know this, healers! What you're doing by hanging on to that crappy waiting-around energy is you're closing your energy off to the option that someone else could walk in and sign up. You're not letting someone else walk into your world that needs you because your energy is clinging to hearing back from that one person. Let it go!

Think about this for a minute. Setting and holding your boundaries like this is going to be such a good thing for so many reasons. It's going to feel so good in your body to communicate those dates or deadlines clearly. "Hey, if I don't hear back, no worries. I'll assume you're a no."

Hopefully, these sample scripts gave you a few ideas for different scenarios. I know it was important for me to practice different ways of saying things.

It helps to have some script ideas at first because it takes you out of that emotional brain and puts you into your logical brain, where you can detach.

If you're stuck in thoughts like, This is what we're supposed to say. This is how we're supposed to respond; *try* not to get stuck there. There are no shoulds or supposed-tos here.

Even with scripts, you have to practice them so they feel authentic. You have to keep trying them and keep having more conversations. So what if a conversation didn't work well or felt weird? Go try it again. Keep working at it because it gets so much more fun, interesting, comfortable, and so much more effective as you practice.

We're gonna be talking about making connections that grow your business in Part 3, and it's one of my favorite topics. What does that even mean when I make a connection that could actually grow my business? I'll talk about those next-level connections, how to have those conversations, what that means, and who you're starting to think about connecting with.

Let's do it!

Part 3

Making Connections that Grow Your Business

A quick recap of where we've been. Part 1: The energy and attitude you curate as you move into this world of getting to know people and really wanting to know them better, and feeling that before you go into a conversation. We talked about that authentic and genuine feeling of wanting to help them build their business. We talked about what questions to ask and about how to listen actively, which is really important. And then how to take that aligned action that establishes you as a super-connector.

In Part 2: The Art of Juicy Conversations, I covered a little bit about how to start a conversation, and for me, that always includes gratitude. Gratitude is always a really great way to start because the vibration and the energy are amped up immediately. I covered how to master that listening-talking dance, how to know what to say in different kinds of conversations, and a little bit about how to close that conversation in the most effective way.

Now, in Part 3, it's about making connections that grow your business. And that kinda feels like a "Well, duh," right? This is exactly what we want to do; it's what we're here for. We want to make and build better relationships that help us build our business.

The only way this all happens is if you're practicing. Please let it be your homework to schedule five conversations in the week. The more you do this and make it a priority, the more you're going to see the magic happen for your business—practice, practice, practice!

The more people you talk to, the better, until you can begin to discern between the kinds of people you want to talk to and weed out the ones you don't.

If I'm not really in it and invested in getting to know that person past conversation number one, I'll never get to that magical point of possibility for my business building. So you have to be in this full-on, don't give up, get to know somebody at the next level.

Networking takes a lot of time, so you don't want to waste it. But some of that is also practice and starting to use your awareness and discernment. Then you can fine-tune, and it just gets better and better. So, I'll cover how to find those better networks where people get it. And after that, how and why you want to become a super-connector, which is one of my super-favorite things!

If you embrace these ideas and mindset, you're gonna see very real results in your community, business, and bank account. Your business will grow.

It's people who give you their credit card, right? It's people who make an introduction to people who give you their credit cards. And so when you want more money in your bank account, and you're thinking about growing your business, you should be thinking about people all day long and how to get to know them better.

That's what this is about. They're either purchasing a product or a service. But either way, it's that person and knowing who they are and what they want that's important.

Chapter 11

How to Make an Awesome Introduction

Making an awesome introduction for your business colleagues and friends

If I had to sum it all up—the secret of networking—that would be it, that first sentence. You should be asking yourself how to make an awesome introduction.

When you have a first conversation with someone, **you might even begin by saying,** "One of my goals today is to make some great introductions for you. To be able to do that, I'd love to know more about what you're looking for and about you. Does that sound okay?" And when they say, "Yes, great," you can say, "Tell me about yourself!"

Wouldn't it be cool if your networking conversations went down in a way that, by the end, you each made one or more introductions for each other? I've been in these kinds of purposeful and directed conversations, and they are a blast!

I'd love to shout out a guy I met recently, Simon Severino. He was a new introduction to me, and I signed up for the "Power Hour" that was listed on his scheduling link. I loved that he called his networking session a special name. Giving it a title, "The Power Hour," amped up the energy right away. So I signed up and read his explanation on the scheduling page, where he was very clear about the goal—to make three introductions for each other by the end of the hour.

It was actually 45 minutes, not a full hour. But hey, "power" rhymes with "hour," so I get it. Whoa, you guys! I've never met anyone so structured and goal-oriented in a networking chat. I really loved that. For me, it was clear, fun, and we were in action together, which made it feel very purposeful and productive.

I want to give you an idea of what's possible here, how you can structure your chats, and how you can teach your conversation partners something powerful.

When I saw Simon's "Power Hour," I thought, *Oh, hallelujah. I cannot believe I have met this guy who knows what this is!* We were typing away as we talked and listened; it was casual and fun, and we asked each other questions about who we were and what we did to help each other think of who we'd make the introductions to.

Simon said something like, "Oh, yeah, you need to meet Bill. I'm gonna do this for you right now." He paused and typed out a quick email introduction for me and Bill. BAM! One intro, done. We went on like that until we'd each made three intros. It was brilliant.

I challenge you all to think about how you're structuring that chat. What would that look like for you? How can you teach people effective ways to network? You can decide what that goal is by the end, and you can teach your partners. What will you do to make it productive and fun?

One of the strategies I love the most is a quick, in-the-moment introduction. They're either made during the conversation or immediately after. So, if I haven't typed one out while talking to someone, you know I'm writing it down in my notebook and doing it immediately afterward.

Six Keys to Making Awesome Introductions

KEY #1: This is key number one to your introductions—they're fast and furious.

Do not wait because when you get distracted or busy, you'll forget. And, remember, it's the intros that establish you as a super-connector. We'll talk a lot more about that in Chapter 15.

KEY #2: The intro is aligned with that person's goals.

Do I introduce my friends to everybody? No, it would be overwhelming and not appropriate. Now, I don't really know what kind of magic could be made if I introduced you to everybody, but I really need to know something about you so that my introductions have a notch of alignment. I'm not afraid of making an "I'm-not-sure-if-this-is-fully-aligned" intro as long as the two people get networking at the next level. For someone who is new to it, I think about it a bit more first.

How do we make a more-aligned intro? Go back to our first couple of chapters and read about listening and asking great questions. If you're asking great questions, you're going to know something about that person, especially what kind of introduction they're looking for. Do not forget to ask that question!

It seems so obvious, but sometimes we miss it. I don't leave a networking conversation without saying, "Hey, Lisa, who are you looking to be introduced to right now?" And if that person isn't able to give me a clear answer, I'm going to keep asking questions until I get clear.

I want to get to know them a little bit better at that point. Maybe a little more getting to know them helps me think of somebody.

KEY #3: It's all energy.

If you haven't already noticed, this introduction is full of inspirational and good-vibe energy. There's nothing negative about this introduction. If you notice a speck of that, pause and re-group. If you aren't already in inspirational energy, motivated, excited, energized, or inspired, stop what you're doing. Because whatever you're going to put into that introduction is going to be infused into the energy of that introduction. I don't need to tell my brave healers this, but sometimes we forget that it's like anything else in life; it's all energy.

Everything is attraction! If you've gone into networking up until now with dread, I challenge you all to stop that today. Be excited. Be in wonder of what could happen with this new relationship. Be in a positive energy, just like you are in all the other ways, and infuse it into that introduction you're making for the person.

KEY #4: It doesn't have to be perfect, just made.

When I make an introduction, it's as informative as it needs to be. Sometimes, I'm in a hurry, and it goes something like, "Lisa, meet Laurie. Lisa's one of my healers, and Laurie's also one of my healers; you guys are both authors, and you're gonna have a great conversation; go!"

Some of you have received quick typed introductions from me because I'm in a hurry, and I just want to get it done. And don't you appreciate the intro, either way? Done is better than not done. I get out of my perfectionism and send intros when I can; otherwise, they don't get done.

But I do try to give a little bit of info about each person so that they each know why I'm introducing them. A great introduction has just a little bit of that, or as much as you feel good including. The "why" of the introduction is a great thing to include.

 **You might say:** "There's bound to be a great collaboration here. I hope you guys have fun connecting."

KEY #5: Make it short, sweet, and powerful.

For me, a great introduction is short, sweet, and powerful. Do not write a book in your email or message. You don't need to. You're gonna start to get tired from that, and your networking partners won't have time to read it. I do these in three minutes or less, sometimes 60 seconds or less. Don't overtype.

KEY #6: Know the difference between a referral and an introduction

It depends on my intros, but some intros are a little bit more like a referral. If I know Lisa provides a service Lori needs, this is beyond the intro. This is a referral, and so sometimes, when I'm making an intro that's more of a referral, I'm going to write it more like a testimonial.

Example: "Lori, you mentioned the other day that you needed some help with healing a very complicated issue. Well, my friend Lisa is a quantum healer. I've experienced her work. It's phenomenal. It's going to take you to another level you didn't expect. I hope you two have a chance to connect."

That intro is different because it's not just connecting for the sake of connecting. In that instance, you have something specific to talk about based on what you know about the two people and their needs.

 If you get this one thing—making awesome introductions— it will change your networking and business game.

As you move forward and have more and more conversations, you'll need to track them. What you track grows. And that goes for everything— conversations, money, awesome magical positive juju, everything! You want to track networking conversations, not just because everything is energy and attraction. You need to track because, unless you have a photographic memory, you'll forget the who, when, why, and how, and you'll need a way to follow up and keep the goodness going.

Let's talk about simple tracking next!

Chapter 12

How to Track Your Conversations

I track my conversations on a basic Google Sheet, and Acuity is the scheduling system I chose at the beginning of this journey because somebody recommended it to me at the time. My Acuity scheduling system is linked to my Google Calendar so that my appointments show up there.

Choose your systems and programs carefully because once you start one of these programs and pour time, energy, and tears into learning it, believe me, you're not going to want to learn another one unless someone convinces you that it's much easier.

I started with Acuity, learned it, and survived. And there's no way I'd change at this point (unless I hire an executive assistant to run the whole thing for me) because it took too much effort to learn.

Many people use all kinds of different scheduling and tracking systems. One scheduling system I hear about a lot is Calendly. For tracking, you may have a system in your CRM (Customer Relationship Management) program, or you may just use a simple spreadsheet, like I do. Don't make it complicated; make it something you can easily access every single day. When you're moving to the next level in your business, and someone else can help with appointments, scheduling, and tracking, ask them what they like to use.

Being an amazing networking partner also means you've updated your systems and technology knowledge so you can easily communicate, schedule, and follow up with people and make it easy for them to do the same. I'm not perfect at this, but I do operate with a learner's mindset and am improving every day. Keep going and keep improving your systems. And this advice comes from someone who used that Day-Timer paper calendar for 30 years, y'all. If I can do this, you can, too! It's just about practicing and getting used to it.

Tracking your networking conversations will be a huge help and is part of the business growth you'll experience. In the beginning, if you track in a notebook, so be it. Do what works. Eventually, when you're having ten or more conversations a week (or several a day), you'll need a way to keep track that is not scribbled in a notebook.

When you really get into this, it gets a little overwhelming. You'll need a spreadsheet. [Says the girl who hates spreadsheets]

I work on a Mac. I opened up my Numbers program and created a spreadsheet that included these fields: Name, Email, Cell number, Date we chatted, Follow-up notes, Follow-up action/Date.

Before this, I tracked in a spiral notebook and put one person per page. But after a while, I found I was having so many conversations I had to leaf back through my notebook to find follow-up steps and info, and I finally sat there and thought: *Oh my gosh, who did I talk to this week?* It was totally overwhelming and not efficient. I'm currently working on typing notes as I go (I let the person know that's what I'm doing so they don't wonder if I'm multitasking during a conversation), and then it can be done right in my spreadsheet.

Tracking shifted everything for me. It's going to be powerful. Get into the new habit of it. Keep it going, and pretty soon, it'll be easy, and you'll just have it up on your computer as you're networking.

Getting Help with Tracking

I know it might be "other level" for some of you to think about having somebody help you with tracking. Because I started having ten or more open LinkedIn messages going on at any one time, I really started to need help. I was dropping the ball on follow-ups, not seeing intros and missing opportunities. I ended up hiring a virtual assistant to track for me and add notes to a shared spreadsheet. And then I could breathe again and check that every couple of days.

I had a regular message I typically typed to respond to an intro, and so that made it easy for an assistant to copy/paste when she saw a new intro. I knew I wanted to reply to this message with, "Hey, thank you so much (name of the person who made the intro) for the great intro. Great to meet you (name of new person). Would you like to set up a chat to get to know each other better?"

This was something I was typing every single time to get the conversations going. What I realized was I could actually have somebody manage that for me. And then, it was up to me to track the follow-up actions. This was extremely helpful.

I wasn't worried that it didn't sound like me because I typed the note. My assistant was just putting it in there for me. When you get to the place where this feels overwhelming, but you realize the benefits, think about getting a little bit of help with your reachouts, responses, and tracking. It will help you take it all to another level.

Tracking Notes and Energy

In terms of conversations and follow-up conversations, you want to remember what stage that conversation is in so that your next one isn't a full repeat of the first. I'm guilty here. I have trouble remembering. Notes are important to me.

Your conversations (and the people you're talking to), just like your money and other things you 'manage,' are like a lover. If you pay attention to them, respect them, and treat them like you would like to be treated, they flourish, and so does the relationship.

With networking, I challenge myself to get into that same kind of mindset, like this is my lover. How would you treat somebody if that were the case? How would you act if this was something you wanted to nurture and something you wanted to grow, evolve, and improve, that you want to get bigger and better?

You would respect it. You would pay attention to it. You would track how it's going. You wouldn't ignore it or stay afraid of it. Check yourself with this networking stuff and begin to shift your mind (awareness, energy, and habits) about it. It will be a mind-blowing shift you didn't expect when you use all the energy and mindset principles you already know and apply them to this!

Let's move to that follow-up now. There's fortune in the follow-up, but only if you set a badass foundation first!

Chapter 13

The Follow-Up: Foundation Before Fortune

I've said it so many times, and honestly, I'm trying to get better at it. It's the follow-up conversations that will create your magic. It could be as simple as a note that says, "Thank you so much for taking the time to talk with me today. I really loved the conversation. I'd love to schedule another one!"

Aside from taking quick action, another sign of being a super-connector is typing out a quick thank you note to that person and making sure that gets done quickly. This puts another task on your plate. However, gratitude is always badass energy to play in, no matter what.

If you made your intros already, you might do a quick follow-up note to let them know you made them and to thank them for their time.

 You might say: "It was really great to talk to you today. I hope you saw those intros that I made earlier. If you have any questions, please let me know! Would you like to schedule a follow-up conversation?"

Remember Simon? We had the power hour, and at the end, before we finished (he was very respectful of my time), he said, "Would you like to set up another power hour?" At that point, I was a *Hell Yes* because of how our time was spent together.

When you meet somebody like that, who not only gets networking and how to make introductions, it behooves you to stick with them as a regular networking partner and see where it goes. In fact, since meeting him, I've rethought networking in terms of always putting time and energy into new conversations. I'm thinking moving back to a core five or ten might be the way to go. We'll see.

Following up was the point here. Set that follow-up date. You could do it with a text, email, social platform message, or whatever. Don't forget to follow up. Return to your spreadsheet. Remind yourself who you talked to.

When I realize it's been a while since I've connected with someone and I have a desire to reconnect, I might reach out and call myself out.

 You might say: "Oh my gosh. We talked like six months ago. I can't believe I haven't followed up with you yet. How are you doing since we talked last? Would you like to schedule another conversation?"

It's okay if you forget. Time goes by. It happens to everyone. Your effort to come back for the follow-up means everything because most people don't.

Lastly, just a reminder that many times, the magic in a relationship happens in conversation five, or seven, or nine. It's so worth the effort of following up with people you enjoy talking to! And that's the key—choose your follow-ups! You won't have the time (or desire) to follow up with everyone. Use your intuition. Who made you feel awesome? Who had a matching excitement and energy? Who did you really want to collaborate with? Those are your follow-ups.

When you find better networks with people who understand networking and relationship building, your world (and business) will change. Next, I'll share about how to find those better networks to play in.

Chapter 14

Finding Better Networks

How do we vet a networking group so we're not wasting our time? This is a big question. I've learned how to be in better networks that help grow my business. But that took me making some mistakes and having some failures. Of course, I don't believe in mistakes or failures, only learning and lessons. Each step and experiment was a lesson or a stepping stone that led me to the next best step.

If I can pay forward some of that learning to you, maybe it will be easier. And I hope to do that for you.

In my Success Champion Networking group, where people pay money to be there every month, it has been suggested we measure ROI (return on investment) in terms of our time, energy, effort, intros, referrals, and dollars.

We can track the kinds of intros and referrals we're getting. Did we see a new client that month as a result of being in that group? You want to pay attention to a couple of things. Of course, you want to see your business growing. You want to see introductions coming in. You want to see appropriately-aligned introductions coming in. And we'd all love to see referrals. New clients are awesome, and in that case, the networking is paying off, and you can easily assess it that way. You know it's working when the bank account starts to move in the right direction. These are all pieces of ROI, and if you're not measuring, how will you even know?

Most of my brave healer friends also know it's a place they love immediately from the vibe they get. Are the people open-minded? Are they heart-centered? Is there a genuine reciprocal wanting to get to know each other? Because this isn't a one-way road, right? And if it's not high-vibe, you can get stuck in a group that actually drains you and weighs you down. That is not the kind of ROI I want, and honestly, I can't afford to be in groups like that. The energy is important.

When I go into networks, I monitor, assess, and decide if I'll go back. Sometimes, it takes a couple of visits, but I don't let it get to the "three strikes and you're out" stage. One or two visits, and I know. I've practiced trusting my gut in an environment and around people. And I use that intuition and noticing for networking. It's really important.

If it's feeling good, and you have some real, genuine people who want to get to know you and are interested in making introductions, you're good to go. Stay where it feels good to you. And then begin to track other forms of ROI.

Vet different meetings. Try them out. Most every organization gives you opportunities to network for free, even if it's a paid program. If you can come in and try it a few times, take advantage of that. When you're paying for networks, of course, understand what you're paying for. You have to assess that as you go.

I've been in multiple networks, masterminds, and groups. They all have different goals, leadership, vibes, and outcomes. I've been in groups with different levels of fees and kinds of communities and situations. I'm getting so much better at vetting them. It took some failures (lessons) to get there.

Now I know what I'm looking for and how it feels right away. I know if I'm receiving reciprocal energy and effort and what the ROI is for that group. It took some practice and experimentation. Don't be afraid to get in and try stuff and see if these are your people. If you're getting those introductions coming back to you, then fantastic.

You should interview the leaders of groups and masterminds. And you can ask to talk to members of the network first. For a couple of the mastermind networks, I asked the leader to send me a couple of names of people I could interview, and I asked them all the hard questions. "Hey, do you think you're getting your money's worth out of this? Why?"

And if you get any resistance from those leaders, then it's an automatic no (for me). The leader should have no problem giving you referrals to talk to. That's already one gold star if they say, "Yeah, sure. Here are some names and numbers. I'll make the intros."

You can network for free. And you can pay (sometimes big bucks) to network. The big-ass expensive places aren't always the greatest places to be. And sometimes they are business-changing. Do your homework. Ask to talk to others. Ask to visit first.

There are so many options nowadays that there's no excuse. You can find great networks to get started in! In the resources section at the back of the book, you'll find some of my favorites.

Being in better networks has meant spending time with people who care about knowing me and what I do. It's meant that the energy is high-vibe. The better conversations I've experienced don't waste time with superficial chit-chat; they go deep and fast. In the networking events that feel "other level" to me, I'm surrounded by people who've been where I want to go and are very generous about helping me meet my goals. The people in these networks have reached a level of business building that allows them to prioritize getting to know people. These people share a learner's mindset, are coachable at whatever level they're at, and are great listeners. They make fantastic introductions and referrals, and they don't believe in competition, only collaboration.

When you play in the sandbox with people who are visionary leaders and understand networking, your life will change, and you'll be challenged to be a better leader yourself. You'll also hit all your upper-limit problems. You'll be uncomfortable, but that's a good thing because it will force you to ask better, bigger questions about what's possible.

When you play in better networks, you'll be among super-connectors. Know what it means to be one and fine-tune that practice. Let's get to that next!

Chapter 15

How to Become a Super-Connector

Here's the why and how of becoming a super-connector beyond taking quick action. First of all, being a super-connector feels awesome, and everything is attraction. When you're feeling awesome, you're living in "awesome" and attract more of that!

Being a super-connector is key to becoming a master networker, not only because of the energy and attraction but because **being connected to people and making great connections, introductions, and referrals to other amazing people is what grows your business.**

Imagine that person you've made an introduction to and their reaction when they get it: "Whoa, she already made an introduction for me. She's awesome."

This is one of the marks of a super-connector—they don't hesitate; they go for it. The introduction is appropriate, aligned, and speedy. I'll say it—it's an amazing manifesting activity to be in every day to connect people to other people who are making their business dreams and goals come true. The more I connect people and aim at being a super-connector, the more awesomeness (love, gratitude, energy, resources, money, and introductions) comes back around to me.

One key to success with this is doing it without the expectation of it coming back around to me from any specific source or person.

I do it because it feels good. Healers understand this. We give, not just to get. We give to give because that energy is in us, and everything is attraction. When I create that feeling and energy in me (no matter how I do it), I'm living that life I dream of.

When I get to be in that awesome feeling, guess what I attract more of? Of course! That awesome feeling. It comes back to me in so many different ways, expected and unexpected.

I love living this way.

How are you being a super-connector? You're making those introductions quickly. You're not saying you'll do it and then not doing it. You have integrity in terms of what you say you'll do. You become somebody they remember because of that, and when they think of somebody to introduce to you, believe me, it'll come back to you.

More Traits of a Super-Connector

I'm an introvert, in case you were curious. Introverts can be super-connectors. I'm a fantastic example. It's not about being outgoing or being an introvert or extrovert. It's about genuinely wanting to get to know people and help them. Which all healers I know want to do, no matter if they're introverted or extroverted.

Introversion is how I recharge—alone. But I love to connect with people. So, I call myself an extroverted introvert.

If you look at the success habits of a super-connector, you'll see they're learned skills and behaviors. You can shift and improve because you can practice these skills.

You might be coming out of your shell a little bit in terms of talking about yourself, but it's not about you.

Here Are 11 Keys (and Action Steps) to Becoming a Super-Connector

KEY #1: It's about how you can help other people.

Don't hide behind your old, conditioned, shy behavior. You just weren't taught the skills. You think you're shy and bad at this, but that's because you think networking is about selling your shit. You had it wrong. It's about helping people. You do that every day! You're actually a pro at this.

You all have been on a self-development journey; you've been doing the work of healing. And for each of you here, that means something different. But what I already know about most of my healer friends is that they have a mission to help others. They just weren't taught how to have "networking" conversations that focused on the other person. We were taught we had to talk about, promote, market, and sell ourselves and our services in those conversations. This isn't about that. You need both skills. But networking is about your genuine desire to help others, something that's already a part of you.

ACTION: Write down the names of three people you want to help.

———————————————————————————————

———————————————————————————————

———————————————————————————————

KEY #2: It's about your energy curation.

Remember my friend Mark Fujiwara, who says: "I only want to talk to +2 people." He put that rating system on the energy he feels during and after a networking conversation very purposefully. If he's inspired and energized, it's a +2.

From now on, when you're having these networking conversations, and you're feeling some kind of negative way about it, maybe ask yourself if that's an old conditioned feeling you're having based on something somebody taught you or some funky experience you had some time ago. What if you could completely flip the switch for yourself and look at this a whole different way?

When you become a super-connector, that's the kind of energy required. I've met potential clients who've become clients, and I've met collaborators, joint venture (JV) business partners, friends, work husbands, and all sorts of other amazing kinds of people and opportunities through these conversations. Keep yourself open to what's possible in terms of these conversations.

It might not all be about getting you clients. It could be about a program the two of you dream up together that creates a whole new business for you. Who knows what this is? Stay in that energy when you meet people—genuine curiosity about what's possible. And be a +2!

ACTION: Add a column on your spreadsheet that helps you assess the energy of the conversations. Rate it from -2 to +2 and refer back for +2 follow-ups!

KEY #3: Networking is a primary business-building task on your list.

Super-connectors prioritize networking. It's on their to-do list as a business development task, and they usually get it done first thing in the day. They may use time-blocking to make sure it's on their schedule. This isn't something they put at the bottom of their list or delegate. They recognize it as the main business-building activity for growth, and it gets done first. A super-connector knows it's what moves a business to empire level, so they prioritize it.

Time to ask yourself if you've been prioritizing this. Is it on your list at all? Do you have a goal for how many conversations you want to have each week (or day)? Now would be a great time to set a goal for yourself. How many reachouts do you want to make each day? And how many conversations would you like to be having each week or month?

ACTION: Block time on your schedule every week for networking. Go ahead and get that calendar out.

KEY #4: Super-connectors make introductions every workday.

Super-connectors who are visionary leader-aliens introduce people all the time. It's always on their mind, grocery store or Zoom; it doesn't matter. And they're always really truly wanting to get to know people in a genuine way, and it shows. Many of my healer friends are actually pretty shy and lean into their introversion a lot. What I want you to know is breaking out of your shell a bit is a powerful strategic business move. And it takes practice.

ACTION: Take five minutes at the end of your day to tally your introductions. If you weren't able to make any, think of one person before you finish up for the day.

KEY #5: Super-connectors ask for permission before they offer advice or sell.

This is an interesting and powerful trait I've noticed in how super-connectors communicate. When they ask permission before giving any coaching or advice or before they share their services with you, it builds trust. This is a next-level skill. They remember to ask before they blurt stuff out. They want their partner's buy-in first to make a great foundation for the conversation.

They might ask: "You've expressed frustration with (a problem they're having). May I offer some advice about that?"

Or another example: "You have a problem that I have a perfect solution for. Would it be okay for me to share about (name of the program or service you offer)?"

ACTION: Next time you're tempted to blurt out your advice, pause and ask first.

KEY #6: Super-Connectors ask questions when they need more clarity to make an introduction.

When I'm talking with someone and asking questions about what they do or who their ideal client is, and I'm not clear about it, I always ask clarifying questions to make sure I understand. This is a mark of a super-connector. They have an interest in being clear about you because that's how they can make a great introduction. They often won't let a conversation fade off without getting the clarity they want or need. A super-connector will ask for a second conversation with you if it's going well, but they need more time to ask more questions and get more clarity about what you do.

ACTION: Get clear enough in your next conversation that you think of someone to introduce that person to before you end the conversation, and write that name down!

KEY #7: Super-Connectors always ask that one question: Who are you looking to be introduced to right now?

They don't ever forget to ask this. It's key. It's the start of being able to make a great intro.

ACTION: Make a note for yourself so you don't forget to ask this question of your networking partners. Put it wherever you'll see it!

KEY #8: Super-Connectors are generous about helping and often offer to share, introduce, or showcase you during the call.

What I've noticed about some "other level" connectors is they're willing to share, make multiple intros, or have you on their podcast, and they offer it during the call. Generosity is always the mark of a super-connector. We are, for sure, over-givers, sometimes at our own fault. But it's always evident when you're talking to a super-connector because your reaction is usually, "Whoa, I've never met someone so generous!"

When I meet someone I want to stay connected with, develop a further relationship with, or who I think is just amazing and awesome, I create ways to help them be seen and heard that overlap with serving my audience. You'll meet people who can help you serve your audience with information or training. I'm always dreaming up ways to collaborate, such as creating a workshop for my audience and having them come in and teach, interviewing them on my podcast, co-teaching workshops together, or quoting them for my blogs or social posts. Giving them exposure to my audience is a big gift for them. I use this as a networking strategy when I want to create a relationship with someone at the next level. There are so many ideas!

ACTION: Think about how you can create an invitation for somebody you want to take the next step with. How can you help them build their business beyond the intros?

KEY #9: Super-Connectors have their tech down pat.

When you meet a super-connector, they usually offer their scheduling link to make things easy. Usually, you'll get an instantaneous email notification with a button allowing you to add the appointment to your calendar. They usually allow you to choose a phone call or Zoom (catering to your preference). They have a follow-up system, and you'll get a note thanking you for your time after the chat. You may notice other things they do (like my friend Simon's "Power Hour") in the scheduling messages that make it easy, efficient, productive, and exciting.

Another tip I learned (as mentioned previously) is to have my contact info and scheduling links ready for every networking meeting I attend to make it super easy to copy/paste them into a Zoom chat for others to click on. Make sure you add the https:// to the front of every link so your friends can click from the chat.

Also, I find super-connectors in networking meetings are taking advantage of that chat and the private chat functions and are setting up conversation dates during the meeting. If you're in a networking meeting, this isn't rude; it's smart, and the leaders expect you to do it!

ACTION: Create a contact info document that is easily accessible during networking meetings so you can copy/paste your info.

KEY #10: Super-Connectors are interested in getting to know you before it's about the business opportunity between you.

I had to be coached on this one because I'm a crazy alien, and most of the time am so intent on not wasting time that I go right for the business talk. But what I've learned from hanging around millionaires and billionaires is they don't care so much about the business. They care about you, believe it or not.

We're used to the opposite. And this threw me at first. I thought people like that, who'd attained a certain level of success, would want to get to business. I learned they'd rather build the relationship and understand who you are at the next level first.

ACTION: Gut-check your genuine interest in this person before you ask about business.

KEY #11: What they do when they can't think of anyone to introduce to you.

Sometimes, you don't have an aligned introduction for the person, or it's just not clear who would be a great intro. It's okay. I've had to give myself some slack on this. I try my best to ask great questions. But if I can't think of anyone, I usually call myself out and ask for help.

 I might ask: "What else do I need to know about you and what you do that could help me understand who I might introduce you to today?"

I will say that to them, and it's genuine, and they can feel it. Sometimes, they have to pause and think, *okay, what do I need to tell her about this?* It might challenge them (in a good way) to explain things more clearly. You just give them a minute to think about it, and they might start a story or talk about something that does spark something in you and help you think of someone.

If I get to the end of a conversation and don't have anyone in mind, I'll typically close with something like, "Thank you so much for spending this time with me today. I've written a lot of notes, and I'm going to think about this a little bit; why don't we set a follow-up call for (date) so we can continue to help each other? In the meantime, I'm going to think about some introductions for you; if you think of anything else you forgot to tell me that might help me, please feel free to email me." Close the conversation in a way that's still positive and lets them know you care about it.

On another note, sometimes, I'll be out and about, or at some other meeting, or somewhere three months down the line, and I'll think of that person. It happens that way! And I'll think: *Oh, I have to introduce them to so-and-so!* Who cares when it happens? Sometimes, you won't think of it in that conversation, or even the second or third, but maybe, who knows, down the line, you might.

ACTION: Remember to take detailed notes each time you talk with someone so you can refer back to them when you need to.

Those are some of the traits of super-connectors. I'm sure there are more you can think of. Who are those people you had the best conversations with? Why?

I'm always noticing what makes a conversation awesome and trying to model after that. I ask: How can I serve them? How can I send them a special thank you or a note? That's networking, y'all. How can I go above and beyond and give the best, amazing service to the people who've already been there and or sent me clients? And then watch what happens.

I saved how to talk about yourself for last because it's the hardest thing. I'm going to cover how to open a sales conversation and how to curate that high-vibe sales conversation energy. I'll share more about how to detach from the outcome, how to know when to stop or proceed in a sales conversation, and how to close a sales conversation with grace and ease.

Let's do it!

Part 4

How to Share Your Business and Offerings Like a Badass

A couple of decades ago, I was outside my kids' preschool when another mom stopped me to say hi. "Hey Laura, how are you? I never got to hear about what you do in our meeting the other day."

"I'm a physical therapist," I replied.

"Oh, I could have sworn you were in sales," she said.

You guys, I was actually offended. Because what I thought of sales was not what I know it is today. I assumed she thought I was pushy and annoying. Today, I understand that when I share my offerings, I'm giving someone a chance to change their life. I feel brave, confident, and excited to share. And if they feel annoyed, that's none of my business.

Let's talk about how to share yourself, your business, and your offerings like a badass. The first thing we need to understand is when the conversation is actually a sales conversation. If you don't know, you'll feel lost. And I want you to feel amazing.

Why do I say 'badass?' When I felt like a badass, I didn't feel like I was trying to sell anything. I felt so good and relaxed about sharing that there was nothing left of that icky feeling. I feel my chest when I type this because sometimes that's where it is for me. Sometimes, it's your gut. It's different for all of you.

I felt like a badass when none of that was there, and I wasn't having a visceral reaction to talking about myself and what I do and actually asking people for that credit card. I wasn't trying anymore; offering the sale felt easy.

Let's do it! You can do this!

Chapter 16

When is it a Sales Conversation?

 Listen up, amazing, brave healers, **"Sales is just a conversation with an outcome."** Thanks to my friend Donnie for that. Don't get all constricted now that I typed the "S" word.

I saved selling for last because it's the least important and gets us into the most trouble. Last is really where sales should be in most of your initial conversations anyhow—last or non-existent. If you've been paying attention, you've been hearing what this is about—helping other people build their businesses by being a connector and making introductions.

Let's talk a little bit about these different kinds of conversations because you don't jump into talking all about yourself and what you offer until you know for sure you're talking to someone who wants that information and can benefit from what you're offering.

Most of your networking conversations won't be sales conversations; they'll be get-to-know-you conversations. Some will turn into sales conversations, but they don't start that way. In fact, starting them that way could sabotage them.

What is a sales conversation? The reason we're talking about this kind of conversation is because it's different than a get-to-know-you. When you have the awareness of the kind of conversation you're moving into, then half the battle is won. If it's a get-to-know-you, you're probably not going to be sharing anything in the realm of your business offerings unless it's natural and feels good to you. And both parties are there to share what their offerings are, but you might not.

Let's talk about the case where someone reaches out to me and says, "Laura, I really want to hear more about the Brave Healer Transformation School. I want to know how to become an instructor. I'm very interested. Give me all the details."

I might get that chat request through my scheduling link. I know going in that this is a sales conversation. They're interested in something I have going on, and they want the details for it.

In all other instances, I've seen my friends get confused. They think networking is always that kind of conversation, but actually, 90 percent of the time, it's not. Networking is getting to know you and building a know-love-trust relationship.

A sales conversation, which might come out of that networking, is when they've already expressed interest and ask for details. When that happens, you have permission to give them the details, including the cost of the program and whatever it is you're sharing.

Somebody might come into my world for that awesome conversation, and they've already filled out the form for my scheduling system that says, "What do you want to talk about?"

I already know they want info about something, so when we get onto the call, **I might say:** "Hi (Name), it's great to see you today. Thank you so much for scheduling a chat. I see from our scheduling note that you'd like some info about the Transformation School. What questions do you have?"

Now, I could have said, "Hey, I see you're interested in the Brave Healer Transformation School. Let me tell you all about it." But I didn't do that. I said, "What questions do you have?" This might feel like a subtle difference, but it's so powerful to allow the other person to drive that sales conversation.

I ask that powerful question, and then I'm going to be quiet and see what the answer is. All I'm going to really do to start with is answer all the questions they have. Get back to that dance of listening and talking.

Below will give you an idea of the different kinds of conversations you might find yourself in.

Kinds of Conversations

I think of networking conversations in terms of the desired goal or outcome. There's the 1) Get-to-know-you, 2) Discover how we can collaborate, 3) Pick my brain about what I do, 4) Share my offerings to see if they're a fit, and 5) Follow up on any of these. There are probably more versions of this as you get to know people.

These conversations can be:

1. Cold (you reached out, or they reached out with no prior connection or knowledge of each other).

2. Warm (you had a connection already and knew about each other or were introduced by someone you know).

3. Hot (they are a direct referral from someone who has knowledge of your services and has recommended you) or,

4. Smokin' Hot (they are already your client, friend, or business partner).

No matter the kind of conversation, we can learn to talk about ourselves in a more powerful way that helps the individual feel seen and heard. Even when you talk about yourself, it's not about you; it's about how you can help them. How do we share what we have going on in the best possible way where we don't feel like we're trying to sell anything and feel good and confident about sharing ourselves?

What comes to mind here are a couple of questions I've often asked myself as I work through the self-development it takes to have great sales conversations: Who taught me it was bad to talk about myself and sell my offerings? When did I learn that this makes me too "sales-y" or "offensive?"

I always come back to this idea when people say, "Oh, this feels icky. This feels sales-y. This doesn't feel good."

 Pause here and take a gigantic pelvic bowl breath, and then read with your whole body: **If nobody knows about what you have going on, no lives will be changed.**

Your important work helps people (and more people) when you share about it in bigger ways.

Time to switch up your mindset about the powerful, profound, magical, life-changing work you've dedicated your life to. I know you know you offer something that changes lives. I know you believe in yourself. And it's time to get better at sharing (selling) it. You're going to get good at it, and it will become a natural, authentic, powerful activity you aren't triggered by anymore. This, of course, takes some practice.

Take the focus off of yourself and put it on them. Ask more questions. See how you can help them.

Brave healers, I want to shift this icky feeling for you so badly. If any of you have that feeling inside about sharing yourself, know I get it. It's so hard to talk about ourselves. In the writing world, it's the bio my authors have trouble with. And don't get me started about the first-time interviewees on the YouTube show. For some people, it's the hardest thing to write or talk about yourself and claim yourself as an expert. We've been taught it's bragging. Some of you were told that to your face as a young person. Makes me cringe thinking about it.

 Pause for another deep pelvic bowl breath here if you need to. **If you can't talk about yourself and what you do in a clear, confident way, no lives will be changed.**

With regards to the title "expert," I want you to understand something. If I'm going to line up and interview 20 people who all do the same thing, and I plan to hire one of them to help me, I'm going to hire the expert. I'm going to hire the person who steps up to talk about themselves in a clear, confident manner. I want to know I'm in good hands. I want someone who claims their expert status and follows through with that knowledge, confidence, and support. You'll need to practice talking about yourself with that energy—the foundational stuff I started the book with.

When is it a Sales Conversation?

When a conversation shifts into an advice-giving or coaching session, it's more of a discovery call or sales conversation, but not maybe a direct invitation to sell. If it's a "Pick my brain" session, I give freely without the expectation that a person will hire me or buy anything. I always remember to ask for permission to share my offerings as a call to action before we move on, though.

I might say: "It sounds like you're excited about becoming a published author. Would it be okay to share about some of my publishing opportunities I think would be a perfect fit?"

When you ask, then it's more of a share, and it feels better.

It's a sales conversation when someone has directly signed up to learn more about a program, product, or offering. You know this because it's clearly outlined on your scheduling system or website, and the link is exactly for that purpose. But beware, this is still a give-value-first call.

 I open with: "I know you signed up today to learn more about our self-publishing coaching. How can I help? What questions do you have?"

What I don't do is go into it and immediately lay out all my paid publishing coaching options right away. I don't know what they want to know. Ask first. Let them drive the conversation. Listen more than you talk.

And lastly, in the middle of a get-to-know-you conversation, things can turn into a sales conversation when you begin to share about who you are and what you do, and they start to ask detailed questions about your services.

What I love to do here is over-give. I love to share what I know and help them solve a problem they have. What I want them to know about me is that I'm grateful and generous, and even if they still want info about my business, I'm going to aim that share more about how I can help them. In the end, if they want to hire me right there, then so be it! That is an added surprise and bonus.

What's important for any conversation is the energy you curate before, during, and after the conversation. It must be high-vibe because it's how you made them feel is what they'll remember the most after you chat. How do you want them to feel? Let's get into curating some high-vibe sales conversation energy next.

Chapter 17

How to Curate High-Vibe Sales Conversation Energy

The energy piece of this is how you're going to set yourself up before you even get on the phone or Zoom. How are you going to curate that high-vibe sales conversation energy before you dial that number or hit the Zoom button? That's really important, and it has to do with—maybe you've guessed it by now—detaching from the outcomes.

I already know it's a sales conversation. They told me they wanted information about one of my programs, and I'm excited about that. I'm excited to share, but I'm pretty detached from if I'm going to get a sale or not today. I really just want to provide value and build trust with that person. I've practiced not getting my hopes up. I've practiced grounding and centering in how I'm serving someone, not selling to someone.

I'm here to provide information about something they want to know about, including prices, and answer any questions they have. But inside of me, I'm not practicing any desperate energy.

If I catch myself in thoughts that go something like *Oh my God if I don't get one more instructor, this is going to fail,* I will stop myself. The "I don't have enough" energy is self-sabotaging as well as conversation-sabotaging. Stop all the mindset crap you loaded this conversation with and go to some neutral, grounded, centered place that will help you help them. That crap has negative energy that'll take you (and them) down.

Detach from outcomes. There are probably a lot of other things we could talk about in terms of how you're curating that high-vibe sales conversation energy. But for me, detaching from the outcome is one of the biggest skills. It's badass. It helps me ground into a powerful energy of service, gratitude, and generosity, which is a much better manifesting energy.

I'm there for them. I'm not really there to sell my stuff. It's a sales conversation, but I'm still there for them. I believe if you take this idea and you run with it, you're going to see everything change in terms of how you're sharing what you're sharing and the sales you make because there will be no pressure-y energy. Everything will feel different and much better.

What makes you feel icky is you feel like you're forcing a sale, or you feel disappointed if they don't buy. Fill in the blank with the feelings you're feeling. Understand your own triggers. Let's get rid of those. Retrain yourself by using your awareness when your resistance floods in.

I'm moving into those conversations detached, with positivity, and energized. I'm super grateful, always. Gratitude energy is high-vibe energy.

"Thank you so much for asking about the transformation school. I can't wait to talk to you about this. What do you want to know?"

And then I'm going to be quiet and wait for them to guide it.

If they have one or two questions and then they're quiet, and nothing's happening, then take it back with another question and ask permission to keep talking. "Do you mind if I tell you a little bit more about my mission for this program?"

Did you guys catch that question? They might have had one or two questions. I've answered them. And now they have seemed to pause and don't have a lot more to say. It was short and sweet, but it's finished, and now I think: *Oh, well, they don't have any more questions. Now, what do I do?*

I ask for permission. "Can I tell you a little bit about the mission I have for this program—my why behind it?" Of course, they're going to say, "Yes, please tell me more." And watch me light up in that why.

If you're not lighting up in your why or your mission, you're selling the wrong thing. If you can get to your why, it will probably make you cry. It matters, and it shows.

When we're having that conversation, and I've asked for permission, and they say, "Yeah, of course, tell me more," I'm going to be on fire with excitement. Here's a response about the Transformation School that actually happened:

"This idea of the Transformation School stemmed from our book collaborations. One of my biggest missions with collaborative books was to have my expert healers teach a strategy in the book for the reader. It made so much sense that they could create a course from that strategy or tool. And I got so excited by the books being a bridge to some passive income for my healers!"

I'm using this as an example; it excites me. I'm happy these collaborations are happening. When they get to feel me, my energy, my why, and my passion and mission, all of a sudden, being involved in that feels really good to them. It's a share that helps them feel good. I'm infusing them with those high vibes.

They feel like there's somebody that cares about what's going on past the sale. I highly suggest you get your why and mission into your sales conversations if you can. That's one of the ways I try to create that high-vibe sales conversation energy.

I want to answer all their questions. I'm going to detach from the outcome. I'm going to be there for them to talk about what they're excited about.

In some conversations, they turn in a particular direction that doesn't feel good. So let's cover what to do in the middle of a conversation when maybe it's not going well, or you're coming up against objections, and it's not so fun anymore.

Chapter 18

How to Know When to Cut it Short and Move On (Objections)

You're in the middle of a sales conversation, and it can go in one of two directions. Maybe you feel like you need to stop the conversation and turn it in another direction, or maybe you're getting all the green lights. It might be time for you to be brave and ask for the sale.

In my example above with the Transformation School, here's the continued conversation that ends up in a call to action: "Now you understand a bit about my why behind the Transformation School. Thanks for letting me share. I see we're getting to the end of our time together today. Would you like me to send you the registration link? Are you ready to sign up as an instructor?"

That's the hard part, isn't it? That's the ask. We get a little nervous about that part. If you have all the green lights ahead of time, and it's feeling good, and you're feeling like you can get to this point and ask if they'd like the registration link, then go for it. The most important piece of this is I'm still excited, authentic, and me.

Some of you brave healers get so nervous about this piece because you haven't practiced it. Just practice. Practice with a friend. Practice it over and over again. It just gets better and easier. You'll get to a point where sharing is going to be no big deal anymore. And you'll be able to do it for all of the different offerings you have, whether they are small, medium, or even high ticket items.

When you believe in yourself and your service, and you're in your why, it's gonna show. Practice that sentence so many times it's memorized, and you feel great about it.

 Remember the giving them permission to say no script? **Here it is again:** "And if this is a no today, totally cool, no hard feelings. You can let me know." When you give them permission to say no, all the pressure is off. There's no sticky attachment. You're not making them feel bad. You're giving them permission to say, "No, it's not really for me right now."

You know what I say after that?

You might say: "Okay, thanks for letting me know. Maybe you know somebody that it would be perfect for. I would so appreciate the introduction."

When you've read these scripts and start to practice when you're in the conversations, you'll start to hear the language, and it will feel natural to respond. Don't get to the end of that conversation where the person said no to you, and then everything about you shrivels—your energy, posture, etc. Keep it exciting. Keep it high-vibe till the end. If it's a no, it's a no. Detach and say, "Next." And then go have five more awesome conversations.

Most of us need to get to talking to a lot more people in general, so we get the practice. Then the no conversations don't feel so heavy anymore. I'm getting there. Some of them still feel heavy to me. I still practice, you guys. It's always going to be a practice.

Certain "no" conversations will trigger you worse than others because you have such high hopes for them. It's our expectations that get in the way and get us feeling all triggered. I've learned to shift my mind to service. What I thought was going to be a sale may turn into something very different. The truth is I never know if the outcome is going to be positive or negative. Why waste time worrying about the negative outcomes and practicing that when I can stay curious and open to the possibilities? What you thought was going to be a sale may turn into a lifelong business partner. You just don't know!

When to Cut the Conversation Short and Move On

Do you all know the example where you're in the middle of this sales conversation, and you knew what it was going to be going in? You've answered the questions. You might've been brave and gotten to the ask. And then they ask you how much the program is. It's not time to panic. It's time to be clear, confident, and upbeat. Don't beat around the bush about your fees, please.

This takes practice, too, especially with higher ticket offerings. You have to practice saying it without the, "Um, well, you know. . ." Don't do that. Practice in front of the mirror if you have to.

When I created my first five-figure offering, believe me, it took practice sharing that fee. In the end, I still felt clear, confident, and upbeat, so all it was for me was actually practicing saying the words. I noticed how I felt each time and where my body was getting my attention. Practicing sales calls-to-action is a great practice in body awareness. This will be one of the great healing moments for you if you let it be.

BONUS NOTE ABOUT SETTING FEES: The thing that gave me the most confidence was hiring a CFO to help me analyze my high ticket fee structure based on my real expenses. When we did the numbers and came up with a fee that felt good, I stopped having a problem sharing it.

But what about the objections?

They ask about the fee; you share the fee with them, and they have an objection. This is the thing you were dreading—all the objections or excuses people come up with when your offer isn't a "Hell Yes!" for them.

Maybe some of you have had a conversation where the person turns into an objection machine. They talk about how they can't afford it. They talk about how they have to ask their husband first. They talk about not being sure about the timing or the commitment. Oh my gosh, the list goes on and on, and I'm not the person who's going to give you a script for every objection. I remember a business coach trying to talk me through every possible objection so I could practice knowing what to say in each instance. It never felt right to me.

You may have heard in other kinds of sales or business training that you should have a comeback for every objection and stay in that conversation as long as possible, trying to coach them through their fear. I see this as trying to wear them down. And I'm a hard no on that. It's been done to me, and it felt so bad that all I wanted to do was get off the phone. That is what "sales-y" is to me.

My version is different. **I might say:** "I'm hearing that this isn't a good fit for you right now. That's totally fine. Maybe you know someone that it's a great fit for. I'd be so grateful if you would give them my name."

When someone has come up with two or three objections, it's ultimately up to you how much time, energy, and effort you're willing to spend with them working through all of them. But in my world, I know there's someone else waiting who's a perfect, right fit, and the longer I spend with someone who isn't, the longer it will take to get to the person who is. "Next!"

If you want to come back with questions, that's great. You can use the time as more of a get-to-know-you. You can get closure from the sales part.

How do you keep going with all the green lights? How do you close? It's really about staying aware. It's the practice you all already do every day. My brave healers are amazing because they show up with their awareness every day, even in these networking conversations. Do not lose the connection to that beautiful thing you have. It matters here, in business, even more. Your intuition, presence, and awareness are the gifts. Stay there in that practice, and then get some closure. Move on. Have another conversation. It's all good.

Why would anyone want to have any extra pressure-y feeling? They don't. There's an easier way.

We can do this with grace and ease.

Let's do it!

Chapter 19

How to Close a Sales Conversation with Ease and Grace

I've already touched on a couple of ways to close a sales conversation. This will be different depending on the circumstances.

Sometimes, the scenario is you didn't give yourself enough time for a full-on conversation. This is a good problem to have.

You get into the sales conversation; all the green lights are happening, and you only gave yourself 25 minutes. It would've been so nice to be able to talk to that person for an hour because they are a yes in your book. And they're about to hand you their credit card. You need more time to give them a little coaching or a little value. And that's fine.

If you're bumped up against another call, all you're saying is, "Hey, oh my gosh, I'm so excited to meet you, and I have some more questions for you. Do you want to schedule another conversation?" And, of course, the answer is, "Yes, please!" So you might say: "Let's get our calendars out right now."

That's the closure. Do not wait. Get another date on the books right then before you leave. If you're getting a lot of green lights, keep track of your time. Because it may just be that you need to hop forward to, "Hey, you sound really excited about this, and I'm excited about it, too. Would you like that registration link?"

Get to that so you still have enough time. Because a lot of the time on Zoom, you're dropping a link in the chat, and they're actually clicking on it, and they're able to have a look right then. Having you there to answer more questions is so cool, and it's going to save you time later.

If you can get to that point and look at the info together, I highly recommend you do that, and you have to give yourself enough time to discuss and for questions.

Ease of closure in a sales conversation is really more about what the circumstance is. Here are some options:

1. You don't have enough time to chat, and you need another date, so you close by scheduling that.

2. They've got lots of objections, and they're a no, and you can feel it, so you get closure by saying, "It doesn't seem like this is right for you," and ask them to send someone who might be a fit.

3. They express interest in your offer and want to sign up. When it's that kind of situation, it's magical when the energy is reciprocal, fun, and easy. You've barely given them a couple of details before they're asking how to sign up. So get right to it and drop the link for them.

4. They express interest but have clarifying questions, which you answer to their satisfaction before they sign up. You might need a second conversation or not. Play that by ear.

5. The get-to-know-you state is ongoing, and there's no pressure to take any particular action besides staying in touch. You realize it's not a sales conversation, so it's great to close by offering to make an introduction for them and/or setting another conversation date.

Whether or not there is a sale, it's still great that you had the conversation. Maybe you learned something about the person, was able to make an intro, whatever. So one thing I always do, even if they're asking for information about one of my programs, is ask them to tell me more about them. I'm not going to leave without having at least a few minutes of that.

You might say: "Sally, I'm so happy you're gonna sign up as an instructor for the transformation school. Thank you! Do you have a minute to tell me a little bit more about your business, how I could help you, or any other introductions you need?

Even in a sales conversation, the super-connector wants to make sure they have just a little bit of the "I want to know more about you" in there. Ask some more great questions and build that relationship further if you have a chance. You might come up with two or three connections you can make for that person in the interim. Do you feel how powerful that can be? You were just in a sales conversation, and now you're going to connect them. They'll instantly see that signing up for your program was the best thing they ever did. At least, that's what I want my clients to feel!

I call it reciprocal awesomeness. I love that.

There's one more thing I want to mention about a conversation that turns into a pile of objections. You may feel confused and start to feel that stuck, awkward feeling inside. And, actually, you already know where to go with it. It's the stuck, awkward feeling that's trying to be your GPS system. You're just not used to checking in with it in networking.

You've got to check in; you already intuitively know what's happening. It feels a particular way. This isn't any different than when you make a decision for anything else in your life. In networking, it's the same thing. Grab this idea by the horns right away; it's a form of conversation that you can call "disqualifying."

When objections start to surface, I've started to default to asking disqualifying questions so I can save both of us a lot of time and aggravation. If you can disqualify a client right up front, believe me, both of you will feel immediate relief, and you can go on to having it be more of a get-to-know-you session.

It might sound like: "Hey Sally, I know you want to be an instructor. It sounds like you're not sure if this is the right thing for you. Let me see if I can help. Tell me a little bit more about your business. Are you actively growing a business right now?"

For what I'm doing in publishing and business building, that ends up being one of my disqualifying questions. If they come back with, "Well, no, actually, I'm kind of in transition," I can easily say to them with confidence, "I want to save you some time here. It sounds like you're not quite ready for this. But if you'd like some first steps, I'd be happy to guide you."

The key here is that I'm disqualifying because of the objections I heard, but I'm still willing to offer support to get her ready to be ready, so to speak. I have a call to action that sounds something like this: "Come on over to the Brave Healer Resources Vault, where I have all these cool business resources that'll get you started and ready to be an instructor or author."

It behooves you to have a free version of support if the sale isn't going to go down and you still want to be of service and offer value. You may realize they're not a fit, but they could be if they took a couple of steps first. If you can disqualify them because they're not right for your offer, you're doing them a big favor. I promise you they'll come back when they're ready, or they'll make an intro or a referral because of how you worked that conversation.

Remember to keep your energy about serving them. You're doing them a favor because rather than just being excited about another client and taking their credit card when ultimately they weren't ready and wouldn't have received the best service or outcome with you because of that, you saved them time and money. That builds trust.

If you take a minute to understand them and their situation and ask great questions in the sales conversation, you're developing trust and a better relationship. They will come back and thank you. And they may end up as your client later on because of that.

What resources do you have for those people? You'll have people who are excited and want to move forward. Be ready to serve them at all levels, and you'll have clients for life.

This is about sales conversations, talking about yourself, and talking about your business in a way that helps you feel really great, that doesn't feel like selling. I promise when you flip the energetic switch of this and get to the other side feeling centered, relaxed, and really good about sharing, this whole thing about networking, whether it's a sales conversation or not, erases all the ickiness.

You can go out there and focus on giving people what they need in terms of getting to know, love, and trust you.

Remember, if you're not sharing about yourself and what you do, if you're not getting out there to talk to people about it, then nobody's life is going to be changed. And that's a bummer. Get good at networking, get good at sharing, get good at listening, and asking great questions. Get good at the art of the juicy conversation. Become a super-connector always with the mindset, even in the sales conversation, of, "How can I help you today?" The amazing energy of that is going to build and expand in ways you can't imagine.

BONUS TIP - Showcase your favorite networking partners

Many times, when I'm networking with someone I'm interested in building a relationship with, I will ask myself: How can I help them get the word out about what they do? I try to think of ways to help them be seen and heard.

Here are some ideas:

If you have a podcast, interview people and showcase them.

If you have an online summit, interview people and/or bring them on as speakers.

If you have a blog, feature their quote.

If you do workshops for your audience, bring them in as a guest expert.

If you have a way to showcase people and their beautiful work, do it. Books are legacy work for me. When I help people publish their brave words and work in the world, their legacy becomes part of mine.

Books are the main way we help you be seen and heard in bigger ways. But the books can always move to bigger and bigger things, like speaking, collaborations, new business ideas and partners, more books, etc.

I love that trajectory. I'm always thinking about how else I can help people get the word out. That mindset is a business strategy. Do you have something in your business model that helps showcase others? If you don't, it's my challenge to you. What could it be? Could you do a blog series where you quote people? That's an easy one, right? Do you do regular social posts where you're showcasing a topic that you teach, but could bring some of your friends in and showcase them with a quote? So easy!

Once upon a time, I had a blog I was writing with love quotes. I went out to my author group and asked for submissions of their best quotes on love. They all submitted, and we had beautiful, collaborative, win-win content.

I posted and tagged each contributor. That's networking. So you can ask yourself:

How could I do that for somebody?

Always remember that you'll attract more of what you're focusing on! Go back to your best-ever conversations and focus there. What went right? Have another conversation with them. See how you can help at the next level.

Remember, it's conversation two, three, four, five, and beyond where magic happens. You don't know what's going to happen, but you're getting to know the person at the next level. And all of a sudden, your conversation goes in a direction, and you're like, "Whoa, we just dreamed up a whole new business together in this last five minutes!"

Go back to the people you've loved talking to, and focus there. If you had five of those people on a regular networking basis, I'm telling you it would be just as, or even possibly more, powerful than thinking you need to talk to all new people for the rest of your business networking life.

BONUS TIP - Focus on your best referral partners

Once upon a time, I made a 12 x 12 spreadsheet (thanks to Honorée Corder), and I worked on noting down my 144 top introduction and referral partners. That's a spreadsheet with 12 kinds of professions across the top (of the professionals who most often refer to you) and numbered 1 to 12 down the left side. My top row might look like this: Editors, Networkers, Publishers, Business Coaches, Holistic Healers, etc.

I started to note the patterns of professionals who introduce and refer to me most often. At first, you might not have 12; no worries. I just began filling them in and kept adding as I went on. The goal would be to have 12 names under each column for a total of 144 names. If you just focused on that one spreadsheet for the rest of your business life, you'd be good—it's a lot of names! I weed people off my list when it's not going in any positive direction or it stopped being aligned, and I add new ones.

The most important thing to analyze on that spreadsheet, aside from if that person is making introductions or referrals, is how you feel when you interact with them. If they are high-vibe, high-character, high-integrity, and high-positivity people, they're helping you be a better person and live your dreams. Be unapologetically discerning when it comes to who's on your list and where you're spending your time and energy.

If they're not energizing, or worse, they're draining your tank, kick them off the spreadsheet and keep going back and focusing on the people who have been an amazing conversation.

Chapter 20

The Important Difference
Between Introductions and Referrals

You're going to hear more from one of my networking mentors in the next section, but one of my aha moments came from Donnie: "Referrals will come from your clients. Intros can come from anybody." I've mentioned this a couple times already, but this is worth repeating.

When I started networking and learning about making introductions for other people, I really thought that meant "referrals." But there was a big fat problem there because I was doing a lot of networking and talking to a ton of people. How the heck could I make referrals to all these people without being their client and really understanding how to talk about them? I couldn't. It didn't feel right. And it wasn't.

So when Donnie dropped that nugget, a huge lightbulb went off. **I can make introductions to just about anyone I think will benefit from getting to know other awesome people.** I'll refer when I can actually personally refer the service I have experience with. And that felt amazing. In fact, I highly recommend it; even if you've had an experience with someone's services for free, you can certainly refer to them. Trading services for testimonials is how you start sometimes.

When I refer to my friends, there's a testimonial-type message being expressed. I will refer based on my experience. I refer when someone has asked me about that specific service or when I'm in a conversation and hear a problem I know one of my trusted friends can solve. The referrals are worded differently than an introduction.

 You might say: "Hey Sally, you were talking about needing a great CPA the other day. I wanted you to meet my friend Michelle, who is an outstanding CPA! I hope you two connect soon."

Referrals are between potential clients and people who can solve their problems, and they are based on you actually endorsing the service, which means you really should have some experience with that person and their services.

Introductions, on the other hand, are amazing for so many reasons. I love making introductions to awesome, high-vibe people who are fellow connectors, business partners, and visionaries. I know these people are in the get-to-know-you mindset and will connect my people with other awesome people. I connect because of the possibility of collaboration, clients, business partnerships, and support. And it's never too late to make a new BFF. There are a lot of reasons to make introductions. You never know when one of those will turn into more of a direct referral or something else you didn't expect.

Since doing more and more networking with more focused, high-vibe, visionary people, I've fine-tuned my strategies to ensure I'm the best networking partner and super-connector I can be. I'm taking responsibility for being a good networker to the best of my ability. I believe that is the mark of a super-connector. There's integrity there that builds trust and badass relationships.

I want every conversation to be a positive, uplifting, and impactful one. I want to be caring, compassionate, and generous. I want people to want to connect with me because I have a reputation for making great connections. To want these things means you're a super-connector. Not everyone pays that much attention to these things.

I'm asking myself how to do this more and more now—how to be a value-add to the visionaries I'm playing in the sandbox with every day. I want to support them, introduce them to amazing people, and refer to them when appropriate.

Everyone wants more followers, but how about those dedicated super fans?

When I think about my goals for growing my business, I think it's cool and fun to have more followers, email list subscribers, and social platform numbers; however, when it comes to what works for the bottom line, it's about engaged super fans and repeat customers.

I'm adding this in here because many of us look out into the sea of possible people to connect with, wanting more and more, without realizing there are dedicated current clients staring us in the face. Start with them. When was the last time you invited your current clients to a networking chat? Never?

That was me once upon a time, too. Not anymore. I'm looking at my current client list, each author in each book, each person who joined a dedicated Facebook group, and I'm wondering how I can start there and get to know people at the next level.

With one group of 1,000-plus people, I will be busy for a while. Then it's about filling in my 12x12 with other visionaries and super-connectors.

Who is in your world right now, already a client or fellow healer, author, or business associate, that you can reach out to to get to know at the next level? Is it time to invite them to a conversation? How can you get to know them at the next level and support what they have going on in the world, whether that's in their business or in their life?

When I created my first round of courses for healers and attracted the first dozen into a BETA program, that was the start. Instead of always sitting around lacking energy, worrying about how I'd get that number to double, I went back to those 12 and asked them for feedback and got to know what they were up to. I made sure to stay in gratitude for these people, especially on bad days when it seemed all I heard were crickets when I shared my offerings. I reminded myself that 12 beautiful people showed up and that I could go back and focus there with gratitude.

One thing I remembered to do was ask for a testimonial. But one more important thing I focused on was what was next for those clients. They took the first course, but if I was going to offer a level two of that course, what would it be? What outcome did those people want?

This focus shifted my energy. And that was a phenomenal way to grow my business because it helped me stay in curiosity, creativity, generosity, and gratitude, which, as you brave healers know, is badass manifesting energy.

When you're networking out there in the sea of billions of people, remember you don't need billions of people to make your business a success. In fact, you probably need much less than that. When you begin to focus on what's already in front of your face, you'll see opportunities like never before.

Part 5

Now What?

It's one thing to read a book on networking, and it's quite another to take action. If you haven't checked out the course yet, you'll find it at BraveHealer.com

In this four-session networking workshop, get ready to hear examples and live coaching that will light your fire about networking.

In this last section, I want to add some professional tips from my friends who've mentored me on this topic, collaborated with me to teach it, and continue to build their empires alongside me in a badass community of world-changers. A learner's mindset is so important in life and networking.

 What if there's something you haven't learned yet that could change everything?

Any one of the golden nugget tips below can do that for you! Enjoy, and please welcome my supporters and friends, Randy Molland, Ginny Robertson, and Donnie Boivin, to this book!

Chapter 21

Networking Resources and Tips from the Pros

I'm so excited to introduce you to a few of the professionals in my network who are amazing humans and get networking at the next level. I asked them to participate in this book with their tips. Read closely—these are some truly golden nuggets that will help catapult what you're doing in the networking space.

Meet Randy Molland

I met Randy in our mutual connection, Justin Breen's BrEpic Network group. When I spoke with Randy, it was like the Universe gifted me what I'd been asking for—someone to help me strategize a give-back component for my business.

Randy is the founder of https://GoBigtoGiveBig.com and is truly changing the world by helping businesses give back to the world in bigger ways and helping non-profits do what they were built to do for the people they serve.

Randy's Story and Five Tips:

When I was 25 years old and starting my networking career, I got put in my place quickly. I had a compelling story to share, but often got caught up in the story and never listened to the other person. This all changed when one lady said to me, "Randy, do you ever shut up and listen to the person you are talking to? I can't stand hearing you talk about yourself anymore."

That's when I took networking seriously and laid out some of the practices listed below to make sure I never put somebody in that position again.

Here are the best networking tips I've learned through my entrepreneurial journey:

1. **It's free to make introductions and be a super connector**

    I learned this from my good friend Justin Breen. After our first call, he asked me, "So, who can I introduce you to that would be of value to you?" I thought it was such a value add to our relationship, and the three people he introduced me to all were contacts who could potentially grow my business. It cost him nothing but a few minutes to make the introductions but made me feel very special and brought me huge value. This is a great way to build a relationship with a potential client or someone who can help move the needle in your business.

2. **Video messages bring personality to a conversation**

    Did you just meet someone new and get their phone number? This hack will help you in many ways. After meeting somebody, I send them a video message thanking them for their time, recapping our conversation, and letting them know I believe in in-person connections, and that's why they got a video message. Not only does this get them to buy into you as a person, but it allows me to go back later if I want to reconnect and learn about what we talked about!

3. **High-quality people refer high-quality people**

    One of the things I started being intentional about was only speaking to people who have high character and high alignment with my core values. What I found is that by being strict about who I spoke with, those same people put value on their relationships. In return, when one of those people makes an introduction, I know right away that the person they're introducing me to is going to be a valuable introduction and a high-quality conversation. On the flip side, low-quality connections typically lead to low-quality introductions and wasted time.

4.   A calendar booking link saves time and headache

When you get an introduction and want to set up a time to meet with somebody, the last thing people want to do is spend time going back and forth asking, "Are you free Wednesday at 1 pm, etc.?" Take the time to set up a calendar invite so you can share that link with them and let them find a time in your calendar that works best. The bonus is you also get to collect their name, email, and phone number for your records if you set it up correctly. And no, that's not an invite to add them to your mailing list!

4.   Always be the first to ask, "So tell me about yourself?"

I was once told, "Be more interested than interesting." This led me to believe that if I could be the first to ask, "Tell me about yourself," then they'd be in the position to talk first and share their story. Not only do I get to learn about them, but I can tailor my story based on what they shared to make sure it's the most effective. Without fail, every time I ask somebody to tell me about them, they ask me to share about myself. This means I set the tone by actively listening to them so they will want to listen to me.

Randy Molland is the founder of GoBigToGiveBig, the singular movement that empowers visionary entrepreneurs to expand their impact and income through strategic philanthropy. A seasoned business leader, real estate investor, and endurance athlete, Randy is no stranger to disrupting the status quo in order to achieve new levels of success. Throughout his personal and professional endeavors, Randy has seen one common truth arise among those who build businesses and lives they desire: when people play all out, they are able to GO BIGGER and ultimately GIVE BIGGER. Today, Randy helps entrepreneurs achieve this mission of serving first through the GoBigToGiveBig community, podcast, and fractional Chief Giving Officer services. https://GoBigtoGiveBig.com

Meet Ginny Robertson

I followed Ginny on Facebook and learned about her On Purpose Woman gatherings here in Maryland. One day, I had a Facebook message from her: "Can I use one of your poems in the magazine?"

I was so honored and excited by that request. Ginny helped me claim my title as a poet that day, but she also motivated me to share more of my brave words. I started attending the local gatherings and practicing introducing myself. I eventually signed up as a member, started speaking at meetings, and then ran a group in Bethesda for years.

Ginny and I share a mission to help women be seen and heard in bigger ways. I'm so grateful for our friendship, connection, and shared passion. In 2023, Brave Healer Productions published her collaborative book called *On Purpose Woman, The Complete Holistic Guide for Spiritual Entrepreneurs.* We continue to create our ripple together, and I'm excited she said yes to contributing to this networking book!

Ginny's Story and Five Tips:

I started my entrepreneurial journey in the mid-1990s. The books I was reading and the advice I received from others was, "You need to network." My networking experience was limited to showing up and representing the large corporation I worked for. It was schmoozing with no purpose other than to let the business community know we were there.

Since I'm now starting a business and clueless about how to network, I read books that tell me things like "networking is a numbers game; you talk to enough people, you're bound to get a few to say yes" or offer advice on "how to work a room." I tried some of the suggested tactics, which felt cold, fake, and unfulfilling. And I wasn't making the connections I needed to succeed.

Through my desire for deep connection with other women, I "accidentally" formed a women's networking group and set it up the way I wanted to network. Something I call "Networking with Heart." You can read about it on my website.

My networking tips come from 24 years of observation and trial and error.

1. **Find networking opportunities that resonate with who you are and what you offer.**

   I joined some organizations in the early days because I "should." It took some time and money to admit it wasn't a fit. My ideal clients weren't there, and the people I met weren't connected to my ideal clients. When I try a new networking opportunity, I pay attention to how I feel in the space and with the people. I trust my intuition to know when something isn't for me, and that feeling usually comes quickly. Other times, I may feel the possibilities of the group, so I'll return and see what happens. There are also times when I show up, and I know I've found my people. It's rare, and it's a gift. Pay attention to how it feels, and trust your gut.

2. **Show up.**

   Once you find a group that feels like a fit, show up consistently. It takes time for others to get to know you and to understand your business. You want your networking connections to think of you when they have a need or hear a friend voice a problem you can solve. Showing up consistently reminds them of who you are. More importantly, showing up consistently is how you get to know others so you understand who they are and what they offer. It's the only way you can support them. If everyone is in that mindset, everyone benefits.

3. **Network from your heart, not your head.**

   Focus on what you have to offer the other person rather than what you can get from them. Be courageous and show up authentically and genuinely interested in others. It's always, always, always about the other person. Ask great questions. Be a generous listener.

4. **Be Curious.**

   Curiosity is a superpower when it comes to making deep connections. Be open to seemingly random meetings with others. Be curious about why this person has crossed your path. It might be obvious, or you might see why years after. Be open to who the other person is. Try to let go of expectations. Explore and be curious about who they are without knowing what you'll find. Be open to what happens. Let go of any agenda and see where the conversation leads.

5. **Follow up.**

This is where many of us drop the ball. We find a group, show up, make some interesting connections, intend to follow up with those connections, and don't. Why not? We don't prioritize and put it on our to-do list. We may not know how to follow up or what to say when we do. I follow up from a place of curiosity to learn more about the other person. It's not the time to try and sell your new contact something. It is the time to see if there is something else to discuss. What might you have in common? What is this person looking to do with their business? Who are their ideal clients? Is there a next step with this person?

Networking is not a numbers game. It's quality, not quantity. If you use these tips, you're likely to make quality connections who will get to know you, like you, and trust you. That's how we decide who to do business with and who we trust with our referrals.

For more info on Networking with Heart, check out my chapter in *On Purpose Woman: The Complete Holistic Guide for Spiritual Entrepreneurs.*

http://tinyurl.com/mr4xvuk8

Ginny Robertson *Connects Women Around the World to Their Gifts, Their Purpose & Each Other.* She supports women entrepreneurs with opportunities for deep connection and visibility.

On Purpose Woman Global Community - Founded in 2000, women who yearn for deeper connection and more visibility are invited to try our free monthly online gatherings and our in-person gatherings in MD, VA & FL.

On Purpose Woman Online Magazine - Founded in 2003, women can find information and resources for their Mind, Body, Spirit & Business.

Real Women Real Purpose Talk Show - Ginny talks with women living on purpose, sharing their gifts, and making their unique difference.

She's also an inspirational speaker, workshop facilitator, and author and was the co-host of the WomanTalk Live radio show on WCBM in Baltimore. She was named one of Maryland's Top 100 Women by The Daily Record, Maryland's premier business, law, and government newspaper.

https://www.opwgc.com

https://www.youtube.com/c/OnPurposeWomanGlobalCommunity

ginnyrobertsonopw@gmail.com

Meet Donnie Boivin

Once upon a time, Donnie and I met somewhere online, and he asked me to be on his podcast. Donnie's podcast was the beginning of his business. You can ask him about that story. After that fateful day, we became colleagues, friends, and business partners. We co-led masterminds together and ended up co-writing two books together. Donnie is a great example of what's possible when you build a relationship with someone, and the results are more than what you expected. Donnie and I have been growing our businesses and building our empires alongside each other for many years now, and I consider him one of my top three networking partners. You've read his name a few times in this book. There's a reason for that. He helped me go from hating networking to loving it and using it to bring my big-ass vision to reality.

Donnie's Story and Five Tips:

Networking was created by broke people. That's the blunt, unvarnished truth that history reveals if you dig into the origins of most networking groups pre-2020. The founders? They were typically folks who'd hit a rough patch, lost a key account, or just couldn't cut it in the traditional sales game.

Networking is often misunderstood as the be-all and end-all for business success. This is a misconception. While important, networking is just one part of a broader business development strategy, not the whole game. It's crucial to distinguish between a referral and an introduction. A referral is like saying, "Bob, meet Sally. I've talked up your services to Bob, and he's keen to chat with you." This implies a sales conversation is expected. An introduction, on the other hand, is simply connecting two good people without any immediate sales agenda.

Your aim should be to make and receive introductions to the right people, in the right places, and at the right opportunities. Remember, genuine referrals typically come from your clients.

Think of it like discovering a great new restaurant. You're excited to share it with everyone. When you provide excellent service to your clients, they become your advocates, spreading the word about your business.

Networking, then, is about building these relationships and creating a network of advocates, not just a series of sales pitches.

Effective networking requires a clear understanding of which industries align best with your own and identifying non-competitive businesses that target the same clientele as you. For instance, consider if bookkeepers are your top referral source. Imagine the potential impact on your business if you connected with 100 bookkeepers in the next 60 days. This focused approach is how you truly harness the power of networking. It's about strategically positioning yourself in a network where synergies exist, thereby maximizing the potential for quality referrals and fruitful collaborations.

Tip 1: Master the Art of Introductions

Instead of hunting for immediate referrals, seek to make introductions. Connect people in your network with others who can help them without the immediate expectation of something in return. By doing so, you become a valuable node in your network, someone people trust and want to reciprocate with. Remember, the most powerful currency in networking isn't money or favors; it's trust.

Tip 2: Adopt the 1 to 5 Ratio

Make sure you're adding value to others before you even consider asking for an introduction. This approach solidifies your status as someone who contributes rather than just takes. It's a strategy that fosters a well-balanced and flourishing network, ready for mutual support. When you do ask for a favor, people will respond positively, not with reluctance. Think of it as the five G's of Networking: Give, Give, Give, Get, Give. Offer four introductions, then ask for one, and follow it up by giving another. This cycle ensures you're always contributing more than you're requesting.

Tip 3: Decode Your Network's DNA

To build valuable connections, you need a solid grasp of your network's landscape. Identify the key players and influencers—the super-connectors. Understand which industries and sectors mesh well with the needs of your contacts. This knowledge enables you to make introductions that are thoughtful and strategically impactful. Think of yourself as a strategic matchmaker in the business world. When meeting new contacts, ask them who typically refers business to them, and be specific about industries. Once you know who they need to meet, take the initiative to make those introductions.

Tip 4: Prioritize Depth Over Breadth

Success in networking isn't just about the number of people you know or the depth of those relationships; it's about who knows you. The key is to develop a personal brand so compelling that others mention your name in influential circles, connecting you with the right people and opportunities. This isn't a race to compile the world's biggest rolodex. Instead, it's about forging genuine connections with individuals who can actively contribute to your business growth.

Tip 5: There's Always Time for One More

In networking, the difference between success and stagnation often comes down to consistency—doing one more thing that pushes your business forward. Always find time for one more outreach, one more introduction, or one more call. It's about understanding that in the world of networking, these incremental efforts accumulate to create significant impact. When you embrace the mindset of 'one more,' you keep the momentum going, ensuring continuous progress and opportunities for your business. This approach keeps you active and engaged in building and nurturing your network, which is essential for long-term success.

Networking is a vital component of a broader business development strategy. It's about building relationships and creating a network of advocates through genuine connections, not just sales pitches. Effective networking involves understanding your industry's landscape, identifying synergies with non-competitive businesses, and focusing on making meaningful introductions rather than immediate referrals. Building a personal brand that makes others want to refer you is key. The art of networking also includes a balance of giving and receiving (the 1 to 5 Ratio) and consistently doing just 'one more' outreach or introduction to maintain momentum. This approach ensures a thriving, reciprocal network that contributes significantly to business growth.

Donnie Boivin, the CEO of Success Champion Networking and Founder of the Badass Business Summit, is driven by a grand vision of empowering numerous individuals to achieve freedom by establishing their businesses. A Veteran, farmer, devoted husband, five-time bestselling author, and award-winning podcaster, Donnie holds a firm belief in entrepreneurship as a profound journey of self-discovery. He advocates that building a business is the ultimate test of meeting and understanding oneself. According to Donnie, the true essence of resilience and determination is found in those who dare to believe in themselves and persist in their entrepreneurial journey, even when others might give up. This perseverance, he asserts, is the cornerstone of true success.

https://SuccessChampionNetworking.com

Okay, now that you've heard from my friends and are feeling even more excited about your strategy, let's cover a few more bonus topics and resources to leave you overflowing with possibilities!

Chapter 22

More Ideas for Networking Badassery

Networking is a never-ending playground. Here are some more ideas, tips, tricks, and extra information to help you stay motivated, inspired, and growing! The next three sections come from blogs I've written on these topics over the years. The first is about ways to support your friends aside from those intros and referrals. The second shares ten ways to talk about yourself more creatively. The third is 12 ways to introduce yourself in 30 seconds. And lastly, when interrupting isn't rude, but necessary.

15 Ways to Support Your Networking Friends, Aside from Intros and Referrals

If you can't make a great introduction or referral for your business or networking colleagues, it's time to support them in the dozens of other badass ways you can.

In our chapter of Success Champion Networking, The Bethesda Badasses, I often feel bad if I can't make great introductions or referrals to my colleagues. We've been at this for over three years now, so thinking of new ways to help them has been challenging. Great intros and referrals depend on the conversations I'm having and the fit with the person I'm talking to. There isn't always a great fit with every single member or their profession or offerings.

Rather than stopping there and giving up, I like to think about other ways I can support them and be a badass at the networking game. In a fantastic brainstorming session in our group, I asked, "What are examples of all the other ways we can support each other in addition to the introductions and referrals?" The list of 15 options we brainstormed together is below.

The next time you're in networking mode and looking for ways to support your colleagues, grab this list and make at least one move! They will thank you for it! And who knows, maybe some magic will be made as a result of your effort.

- Comment on their social post.

- Lend an ear when they are struggling.

- Be a client, if that is appropriate.

- Have them as a guest on your podcast.

- Be an incredible guest on their podcast.

- Subscribe to their email list.

- Write them a testimonial.

- Help them with market research for an offering they are creating.

- Subscribe to their social channels.

- Join them at a live event or happy hour.

- Collaborate to offer workshops or other events.

- Share media opportunities with them.

- Help them BETA test an offering they are creating.

- Create an affiliate partnership with them.

- Share their social platform, group, or offerings.

There are so many more ideas than these 15, but this is a great start to get you thinking and being an excellent networking partner.

One thing I know for sure is that the networking community I've invested my time, energy, and effort with has been worth it. The members have become friends and business partners, and the energy of our group has expanded and grown into something much more than I expected. This happens when all members take ownership of their part in the magic.

Next, in networking, it's always great to be able to talk about yourself in creative ways, especially when you do a lot of networking and it's starting to feel a little boring to introduce yourself, in the same way, every time. Here are some tips about that.

10 Strategic ways to talk about what you do so people can refer to you faster

Explaining what you do or what you need in a way that prompts the person you're talking to to think of someone they can introduce you to is a skill worth mastering in the business development game.

It's also key in terms of understanding other people's businesses so that you can refer to them.

This requires you to have a handle on who your ideal client is, what you do, what problems you solve, and exactly how you solve them.

You have to be able to articulate these things in a clear, passionate way, not only to motivate others to want to help you build your business but so that they actually *can*. People want to help you. You must help them help you!

You'll also want the answers to these questions so you can get super clear about what other people need to grow their business. This list might be more important as it relates to the information you need about others! Don't forget that part! It's crucial!

The following fill-in-the-blank statements will be great information for you to practice sharing and for you to gather about your referral partners.

Get out your notebook and write the answers down! Practice sharing them in your conversations and practice asking the same questions of the people you're having conversations with!

Here are ten ways to talk about what you do and ten things you'll want to know about others' businesses so you can receive and give the best referrals faster!

VISION

• The big vision for my company is _____.

Another nugget from my friend Donnie Boivin was, "Your vision has to be big enough that other people want to help you achieve it." I loved that. Can you state your big vision in a way that motivates people to want to make introductions and referrals?

Flip this to a question for your conversations: What is your vision for this company?

EXPERTISE

• I'm an expert at _____.

Steve Harrison did an exercise with us in his Quantum Leap coaching program that blew me away. Stepping up as an expert in your field is a must. He helped us claim our expert status. And when people hire others, they want the expert they're confident will solve their problem.

It's important to claim your expertise and help people understand just what you can do for them and how.

Flip this to a question for your conversations: Tell me about your expertise!

WHAT YOU DO

• People hire me to _____.

If you're not fully clear about exactly what you do, this will be a difficult business development road for you. What do people hire you to do? What I want you to think about here is a tangible takeaway, not the magical "how" of what you do. What result do your clients want? What do they hire you to do for them?

Use the last two questions for your conversations: What results do your clients want? What do people hire you to do for them?

IDEAL CLIENT

- An ideal referral right now is _____.

Right now, in my business an ideal referral would be a female physical therapist (or other healthcare practitioner) who has her own practice and is also a blogger or writer, but has never published a book. She has an interesting story and is always saying how she'll write her book one day.

Did you naturally think of your own physical therapist, personal trainer, nutritionist, or massage therapist? If I got you to think of an actual person in your life, *score!* And that's the goal here. To help others think of an actual person to introduce you to.

Flip this for your conversations: What's a perfect referral for you right now?

Bonus tip: If you can't think of anyone after the person tells you the details of their ideal referral, ask clarifying questions until you can!

PROBLEMS

- People I work with are struggling to _____.

The healers I work with are struggling to share their message out loud in a way that people really get it and resonate to the point they know they want to work with that individual. Their social posts and blogs are getting little engagement, and they're frustrated about their copywriting getting them nowhere. Their frustration is showing up in an empty schedule, decreased income, and arguments with their spouse.

If you know your own ideal client's biggest struggles, you're going to help others think of someone with that struggle. You have to understand what keeps them up at night. And you have to get to the emotion of things here.

Flip this for your business development conversations and ask your person: What are the biggest struggles for your clients?

WHAT YOU HEAR

- People I work with are saying things like, _____.

There's nothing more powerful than understanding what your ideal clients are actually saying in their day-to-day lives about their issues. How would you know? No, you can't hide out in their homes or plant recording devices. But you can actually talk to them and interview them about it! You will actually hear them say the words that might end up on your sales pages. The best homework I ever got from a coach was to sit down with one of my ideal clients and pick their brain about their life as it relates to my services.

Flip it for your conversations: What are your clients saying in their daily life about this?

WHAT YOU'RE GOOD AT

- One of my favorite problems to solve is _____.

This is a tweak on the "problems" one. It's very cool to know what you're good at and what your favorite problem is to solve. Like, what problem could you solve in your sleep? What do you already write, teach, and speak about? What do you have the code or secret formula for?

Flip it and ask your person: What is one of your favorite problems to solve?

TESTIMONIAL OR CASE STUDY

- One of my clients was able to _____.

Lastly, can you talk about what you do in story form? What is an example or story you can tell about a client who had an outstanding result after working with you? When you tell stories, it's a fun, more entertaining way to talk about what you do as it relates to real-world results your clients have experienced.

STATS

- I've helped _____ people do _____.

Another form of testimonial-like information is how many people you've helped solve a problem. Have you counted it up? Do you know the statistics?

In the last three years, I've helped over 1000 health and wellness practitioners become Amazon bestselling authors. That was a fun stat to look up as an example for you! I'm patting myself on the back for that one. What's a stat you can celebrate today?

Flip it for your conversations: How long have you been in business and how many people have you worked with?

FUN

- When I'm not at work I love to _____.

I could have opened this section with this one because when you get to know someone at another level, you're creating deeper relationships with people and building the know-love-trust factor. What are you sharing with others about your life and passions? Are you keeping your non-work life a secret? Why? When I know what you love, I'm more apt to want to hang out and get to know you better. I'm more inclined to take our business relationship to a deeper level and build that interest and caring required for badass business building.

Flip it on your conversation partner: What do you love to do outside of work?

You all know there are more than 10, right? This is a great start, though. Use these questions with a partner as practice. Find a buddy and go through them with each other. Help each other get clearer, both with the information and with articulating it.

Don't get stuck in perfectionism here. Go out and fail. Then have another conversation and do it better the next time. It's the action that'll help you get the clarity you're craving in terms of answering all these questions for yourself, and getting better at teaching others how to talk about you.

An empire grows as the business owner moves out into the world to share their big vision out loud, but it grows faster if that business owner focuses on helping the people around them build their businesses. Teach others how to talk about what you do. Learn how to talk about what other people do. Be genuinely interested in knowing others and their deepest desires. Be passionate about sharing yours.

These badass conversations turn into friendships, business and referral partnerships, and powerful collaborations when you're practicing being an active, engaged listener *and* an articulate, confident speaker. It's a beautiful dance, a give-take, and an authentic passion.

Master this art and watch your business grow into an empire that leaves a legacy and changes the world.

Next, let's talk about the networking you're doing in meetings with multiple people when you have a very short few seconds to introduce yourself! When you craft a powerful 30-second intro, it should leave people wanting more and taking action to schedule a chat with you!

12 Powerful Ways to Introduce Yourself in 30 Seconds

The world is online, and I love the opportunities right now! I've taken full advantage of all kinds of online networking groups during the last few years, met all kinds of amazing people, and grew my business as a result.

There's a lot to learn in this big, badass world of effective business-building and relationship-making, isn't there? Like introducing yourself in a few seconds in a powerful enough way to pique people's interest enough to want to know you better.

In the weekly meeting I run for my Bethesda, Maryland peeps, we started by crafting a 60-second introduction. As the meetings proceeded over the months, we realized we needed to make those intros shorter, sweeter, and more powerful so we could get to the badass business of getting to know each other in our roundtable discussions and breakout rooms.

What an incredible learning experience it's been to get everything about what I do into a 30-second elevator pitch that's powerful enough to wake up the members who've heard it a hundred times already and still deliver information about who I am and what I do in an effective way to those who don't know me as well.

It's like when you craft your shorter speech or talks; it takes some skill to get it all down in the fewest words possible and have people not only paying attention but wanting to set up a virtual coffee with you. And that's the real goal: Introduce yourself in a way that has people reaching out for that next conversation!

In the spirit of doing that in new, creative, badass ways, here are some of the ideas we came up with in one of our meetings to help spark your next 30-second introduction. Networking hosts, feel free to use our awesome list the next time you run your meeting!

Generally, when you're introducing yourself, you're helping people understand who you are and what you do in a way everyone can understand. If a fifth grader doesn't get what you do, chances are others will be confused. Let's take this further now, though. Here's what to add to that "who you are and what you do" part of your intro to make it unique:

- Add a line or two about **why** you do what you do. It's the passion that will make the difference.

- Tell us how you help people.

- Give us a practical tip or nugget we can take with us regarding your area of expertise. This is my favorite.

- Share a passion you have outside of work. When you realize your colleague also loves to climb mountains, you might hop on a call quicker than usual to discuss!

- Talk about a recent client success you had.

- Give them an idea about what your ideal client would be saying out loud to their friends in terms of the problems or struggles their having.

- Add a little note about your favorite (fill in the blank). Examples: Color, restaurant, car, place to travel, etc.

- Add a sentence or two about how you help your clients feel like a rock star.

- Tell us what "success" means to you in your business, aside from more income.

- Add something interesting that people may not know about you.

- Tell us how you empower your clients.

- Tell us the best thing about doing what you do.

Above all, have fun with your introductions. Relax. Be yourself. And—practice does make perfect. One of the former members in our group used to open his intro up with his "Five words of the day." We not only love hearing those five words, we grew to expect them from him. Whether he knew it or not, he began branding himself when he regularly offered that as part of his intro.

What would be part of your introduction that would help people think about you in a particular and badass way?

The next topic is something my healers aren't too comfortable with but need to get better at. We all have to protect our time and energy, but when you're the leader of a networking meeting, others rely on you to do that for them. So whether we're talking about a one-on-one conversation or moderating a meeting with multiple people, let's get into how to interrupt people in the best possible way when necessary.

When Interrupting Isn't Rude, but Necessary: Meeting Moderation 101

If you lead a community and run events for your members, and you're in charge of holding and managing a safe space in meetings for your members to interact, communicate, express themselves, and learn, then understanding your role as a leader and moderator (and the need to interrupt someone) is crucial.

I've been running meetings, workshops, and interactive events for a long time. I remember someone sharing feedback about a meeting we attended together and the person leading it:

"Nobody held him accountable for taking up all the space in the meeting. Nobody was willing to interrupt him, and that started to feel very uncomfortable. If the leader of the meeting can't control what's going on, then I don't know if I want to be there. It doesn't feel safe."

Great leaders facilitate great leadership from others. We're all leaders. But we're not all practiced at great leadership skills. One of the most important things a leader models, especially in a meeting with her colleagues, is creating a safe, creative, inclusive, accepting, and dynamic space for others to share their ideas.

The next most important thing a leader does is make sure all voices are heard and that each voice is given a fair shake of time without taking over everyone else's time. Time and energy vampires tend not to be practiced in the respectful pause or in the crucial skill of active listening, both necessary for productive meetings and interactions. So it's the leader's job to pause those people and help them with some awareness. In a one-on-one conversation, you may have to protect your own time with a gentle interrupt.

I agreed with my friend that day we discussed this:

"I hear you. Nobody took responsibility for keeping the meeting on track, so it started to feel like a waste of time."

I wonder how much time is wasted in meetings because nobody's willing to respectfully interrupt someone for fear of being the bad guy. Over the last few years, my patience has worn thinner on this topic. Life is short. We have important, world-changing work to do. Working with a team is already challenging without the additional stress of having to police one person taking up all the oxygen in the room and not respecting their colleagues by denying them a chance to speak.

As a leader, it's not only *not* rude to interrupt someone, but it's necessary to make sure you keep your colleagues safe. When you're looked up to as the leader or moderator, your meeting participants will rely on you to practice those skills. I liken this to being an 'awareness monitor' to keep people aware of the fact that they haven't stopped talking, are repeating themselves, or aren't giving others a chance to speak, ask questions, or make comments.

Many people I speak to are afraid to interrupt others. "I don't want to be the bad guy," they say. They consider it disrespectful, so instead, they allow a person to go on speaking without pausing and without taking into consideration the rest of the participants in the room. But when you're on a schedule, with an agenda and a goal, and there isn't enough time for people to share drawn-out comments or opinions, you must be able to gently, respectfully, and effectively interrupt. It isn't about you or what they think of you; It's about maintaining a safe and productive space to work or productively interact.

 Here are three scripts to use when you need to respectfully interrupt and keep your meeting running smoothly:

1. "Please pause a moment. I need to keep us on track."

2. "Please hold that thought."

3. "Please pause. Let's do this. To keep everything running smoothly today. . ."

Then, you can follow up with a sentence to help the person feel seen and heard and place a bookmark where you paused them so that, if needed, they can come back to you or the group at a later time with the rest of their thoughts.

It's important to offer that option for further communication to the person if they should need or want it. You're not there to shut people down. You're there to make sure they're heard and that everyone else in the room is, too.

There are many more versions of the gentle interruption and ways to very respectfully add awareness to the moment when someone is taking up all the space in the room. It takes some practice. But it's worth the effort.

I remember a comment I heard from another friend in a networking group we attended:

"I loved how the moderator of the group ran things. The meeting was on time, and I felt like our time was respected and that everyone had a chance to contribute. Some great ideas were shared, and then we could set up follow-up conversations for the topics we wanted to continue later. We got so much done!"

Yes! That's how meetings should feel!

In my author communities, we often facilitate groups of 25 or more people at once. We have a lot to get done in a short amount of time. We rely on our participants to be active listeners and engaged contributors. We honor and respect every human showing up to those events and greatly appreciate their involvement. The energy starts with gratitude and ends with gratitude. In between, we practice a dynamic and mindful environment that helps everyone feel like they're part of something powerful. The results are books (and communities) that are waking the world up to what's possible.

What if every meeting you led (with one or many people) created that kind of result?

Chapter 23

Your Next Networking Steps and Resources

Your next steps will depend on what your goals are and where you're at in the process of building your network, relationships, business, and community.

Do you need to set up your scheduling and tracking systems?

Do you need to refine your system or process of scheduling, having conversations, and follow-ups?

Do you need to find new networking groups?

Do you just need to get out there and practice?

Wherever you're at, that's a good place to take action! You won't feel the clarity, confidence, or courage first. You must get into action to feel those things. They are the result of the action.

Let's get you to some resources that can help!

Resources

Networking Organizations

For Brave Healers

Don't miss The Brave Healer Monday Morning Superboost with host, CEO of Brave Healer Productions, Laura Di Franco—hey, that's me!

You'll find those events in our Facebook group for healers here: https://www.facebook.com/groups/YourHighVibeBusiness

We have fun a couple of Mondays each month and offer free business development and networking for holistic health and wellness practitioners. Bring your business questions, connections, and networking badassery for this 90-minute inspirational session that includes a speaker's showcase and speed networking. Join the Facebook group for the event invite and Zoom, or email Laura at support@lauradifranco.com for the Zoom link!

My Sponsors

The people who helped contribute their tips to this book each have powerful groups you can be a part of. Remember to vet each group and its founder to make sure it's the right fit for you. I highly recommend these groups for their high vibe, high purpose, and high character attributes.

The On Purpose Woman Global Community Gatherings can be found at https://OPWGC.com

Founder Ginny Robertson hosts multiple online and in-person gatherings throughout the month. You can attend for free. Members receive special benefits like being able to write for the On Purpose Woman Magazine, discounts on magazine advertisements, and featured speaking spots.

The Success Champion Networking family can be found at https://SuccessChampionNetworking.com

Founder Donnie Boivin runs a global community of networking chapters that each meet at different times and days of the week. You can attend a meeting for free up to two times. After that, membership benefits include weekly training, yearly conferences, and speaking opportunities.

The Go Big to Give Big community can be found at https://GoBigtoGiveBig.com

Founder Randy Molland runs a mastermind networking group of business owners looking to give back through their businesses. Go Big to Give Big is a movement that inspires a new style of entrepreneur who believes in mixing philanthropy and business to make a bigger impact on the world.

Other Organizations to Explore

The BrEpic Network is for you if you're a visionary entrepreneur who is out to serve humanity. You'll find Founder, Justin Breen and the organization at https://brepicnetwork.ck.page/

To talk to Justin about the group you'll need to take the Kolbe test. This is a group of next-level visionary leaders and super-connectors, and Justin vets this group heavily. This group will change your business game.

Speakers Playhouse by Founder, Kimberly Crowe can be found at: https://entrepreneursrocketfuel.com/speakers-playhouse/

This is a wicked-cool 90 minutes of electrically fun, free, delightful, gamified networking with other amazing speakers! Join in with people like you who are here to make a difference.

The National Association of Women Business Owners can be found here: https://www.nawbo.org/

Imagine a community of female business owners here to help you succeed professionally and personally. We do just that by way of events, educational programs, and our sisterhood that uplifts, nurtures, and promotes women leaders like you. NAWBO has regular online and in-person networking events. Check their calendar.

JV Connect can be found here: https://www.jv-connect.com

Founded by Michael Whitehouse, JV Connect is an opportunity to achieve three months' worth of networking in just two highly intentional days. You can meet strategic partners, mentors, resource providers, and even prospects. This quarterly dedicated virtual networking event is focused on online business but is a great resource for everyone in business. JV Connect uses focused breakouts and other programming to maximize the number of quality connections that participants can achieve. JV Connect runs in March, June, September, and December. Check the website for exact dates.

Scheduling

There are many systems to explore when it comes to scheduling your appointments. Research a few and then choose something that feels right for you. They will all have a bit of a learning curve, but once you get over that hump, you'll be happy to dive into the world of online scheduling.

Acuity: This is the system I use. Find them at: AcuityScheduling.com

Calendly: This system is used by many friends. Find them here: https://calendly.com/

And in an article that reviewed some of the best scheduling apps of 2023, here's what they came up with (Acuity was included).

Picktime, Square Appointments, SimplyBook.Me, Book Like a Boss, and Zoho Bookings.

Other Helpful Apps and Info

Tracking

If you're going to break out beyond the good old notebook, a simple Google Sheet or Numbers spreadsheet will do. The bottom line on tracking—do what works for you.

Virtual Assistance for Tracking and Networking

As my networking activities have become more robust, I started to feel overwhelmed and decided to get some help with my tracking, especially with PR introductions and podcast guesting being a very frequent activity. It's amazing to have an executive assistant who can provide some virtual assistance on platforms like LinkedIn or Messenger systems and help you keep track of what's happening where.

There are some very highly qualified virtual assistants out there, but you have to do your due diligence and find the right ones. Here are a couple of companies I love to get you started. By the way, you can be getting some assistance for so many other tasks that are bogging you down and keeping you from the business development activities you know you should be doing. Delegating these tasks is one of the most important business growth strategies!

Projects Made Simple, LLC ~ your small business assistant

We create elegant business solutions from the center of our lives to help simplify yours. As a virtual assistant team, we provide day-to-day support worldwide. Dedicated to promptly meeting our clients' needs with meticulous attention to detail, we empower small businesses for success. We tailor our services to suit our clients' unique requirements, regardless of where they are in their business journey. So, if you're seeking assistance or feeling stuck and overwhelmed, our consultation is free. With a few new ideas, we may be able to help! https://projectsmadesimplellc.com

Well Aware Inc.

Well Aware provides virtual assistance as well as time and operations management consulting. Their virtual assistance team has handled everything from cleaning inboxes to engaging and posting on social media to creating content, finding leads, managing calendars, updating CRMs, and much more. Not sure where you need help? Well Aware's consulting arm can provide you the guidance on where it makes most sense for you to start delegating. The company charges by the hour, with no minimums meaning you can work with them at your own pace. https://www.wearewellaware.com

Your Jo Team, Virtual Business Services

Helping small business owners through expansion and growth by taking care of projects and tasks that have been on their list of needs for more than two months. Serving nonprofits through meeting transcription and minutes, with services extending into efforts in equalizing digital accessibility throughout all communities.

Find Jodi on LinkedIn:

https://www.linkedin.com/in/jodi-davis-gonzales-she-her-322417a/

A Rampage of Gratitude

There are so many thank yous to give.

To Donnie Boivin—thanks for helping me love networking, so much so that I decided to write a book about it. Your support and inspiration means the world to me.

To Kelly Kaschula—thank you for the brilliant book design! Your talent and ability to take my vision and bring it to life in the form of art on and in our books is so appreciated. Thank you for understanding and believing in the mission and being by my side to help me bring it to the world!

To Randy Molland—thank you for taking what was in my heart (giving back) and actually creating a strategy for it that helped me make it a reality. This is world-changing stuff, and I'm honored to be on this journey with you.

To Ginny Roberston—thank you for nudging me along, from the very beginning of our first meeting, to be seen and heard in bigger ways. Your sisterhood and friendship are so appreciated. I love being on this grand ride with you.

To Maggie McLaughlin—our publishing pro, thank you for everything you do behind the scenes to make sure every launch goes off without a hitch. I'm so grateful for your support and expertise.

To the Brave Healer Book Launch Warriors—all the people who said yes, and keep saying yes, book after book, to helping us get these brave words into the world in a bigger way, my thanks here won't feel like enough. You're the reason we do this the way we do it. Thank you so much for believing in me, my mission, and this company. Thank you for being part of this world-changing community.

To every person who said yes to having a networking chat with me and showed up to make magic—thank you. These connections and our ability to help each other do the good work we're doing in the world is how we are (and make) the change. This is big-potatoes stuff! I'm so proud of us!

A couple of last words to inspire you:

Everything has been done, said, written about, and created before. . .

. . . but not by YOU!

Your message, brave words, and work in the world matter. That fear of not-good-enough? It's boring.

 This isn't about you. It's about the lives you'll change (or even save) when you share yourself and your business with the world.

It's time to share your work with the world in a bigger way. It's time to learn how to talk about what you do and share that with people as you build better and stronger relationships with business partners who get it. Be brave!

I'm one of your partners!

We don't do this alone. Reach out if you need some help.

And carry on with your healing badassery!

Big love,

Laura

About Laura Di Franco

I was born in San Francisco, California, grew up in Marin County, and went to San Francisco State University, where I played two years of soccer. I moved to the East Coast right after physical therapy school to be with my boyfriend (now ex-husband). I was the first in my family to ever live anywhere else but California until recently, when my sister and mom both moved close to the area I'm living in now—Bethesda, Maryland.

I spent the first half of my life as a severe introvert, extremely shy, and unable to feel worthy enough to be full-on self with people, network, or speak about myself in any way that felt good. Being an athlete saved me during the first half of my life. That's where I belonged and excelled. I was a soccer player, became a marathon runner, and later earned my black belt in Taekwondo. I'm a lifelong lover of figuring out what my body is capable of. That served me well when I became a holistic physical therapist and started helping others heal.

I can say with confidence that every single event in my life served me well. I don't have any regrets or wishes to do things over.

I'm happy to say things have changed in the "shy" and "introvert" departments. While I'm still a traditional introvert (I recharge with alone time), I happily call myself an extroverted introvert these days. My last decade was more about finding out what I'm capable of in the mind-soul areas. This pursuit changed everything for me. I've mastered my mindset, and that continues to create miracles.

Shifting from physical therapist and healer to publisher in 2020 was one of the scariest moments of my life—one of my identity crises. Even though Brave Healer Productions was founded before that (2016), I didn't claim "publisher" until more recently, and it took a huge leap of faith to let my PT hat go. And it was the best thing I've ever done.

What, exactly, was the best thing I've ever done? Following my joy, passion, and soul and following the obvious breadcrumbs the Universe was leaving me. I'm so glad I was brave enough to take the leap.

Because here I am, writing this note to you in a book about networking, something that helped me build this community of expert healers and teachers who are changing the world together. It's amazing. I'm so grateful.

There's more "about me," but if you want to know more, I invite you to connect and schedule a chat. What I know for sure is that the incredible empire that is Brave Healer Productions was built on the spirit of connection. And I can't wait to connect with you!

For inquiries about our free networking events, next collaborative book project, writers' retreat, writers' circle, course platform, or online and local events and workshops, find everything at http://BraveHealer.com

Other books by Laura Di Franco

Good Vibes 365: Practical Prompts for Awareness, Writing, and Transformation

How to Have Fun with Your Fear

The Brave Healer Business Mindset Transformation Journal

Brave Healing, a Guide for Your Journey

Living, Healing, and Taekwondo: A Memoir to Inspire Your Inner Warrior

Warrior Desire, Love Poems to Inspire Your Fiercely Alive Whole Self

The Ultimate Guide to Self-Healing Volumes 1-5

Love Warriors, The Conscious Expert's Guide to Healing, Joy, and Manifestation

Mindset Mastery, Awareness, Meditation, Mindfulness, and Manifestation for the Spiritual Warrior

For a complete list of books published by
Brave Healer Productions, Brave Kids Books,
and Brave Business Books
visit us on the websites:
BraveHealer.com
BraveKidsBooks.com
BraveBusinessBooks.com

Connect and network with like-minded brave healers in our Facebook group: Brave, Badass Healers, a Community for World-Changers!

Your words change the world when you're brave enough to share them. It's time to be brave!

SCAN ME

Get access to The Brave Healer Resources Vault with thousands of dollars worth of training, masterclasses, and workshops that will take your writing, publishing, and business-building to the next level!

www.ingramcontent.com/pod-product-compliance
Lightning Source LLC
Chambersburg PA
CBHW071151120626
46546CB00006B/2212